PRAISE FOR BRIEANE OLSON AND *CO-CREATED*

"*Co-Created* by Pacsun CEO Brieane Olson is an intimate description of corporate culture change that has led to the (co)creation of one of the most amazingly successful clothing and accessories brands today. Olson's refreshingly honest writing style describes both early pitfalls (leading to a chapter 11 restructuring) and careful strategic rethinking to go from a surf-and-skate retailer selling other brands to an own-brand company which puts authentic community building front and center. This book details the secrets behind what I call the First Law of Customer Centricity: Build from the outside-in rather than sell from the inside-out. This is a must-read for both legacy brands needing transformation and all companies who seek to understand the power of next-gen audience marketing."

—Rohit Deshpande

Baker Foundation Professor, Sebastian S. Kresge Professor of Marketing Emeritus, Harvard Business School

"In *Co-Created*, Brieane Olson offers more than a story of Pacsun's reinvention—she presents a masterclass in authentic, purpose-led leadership. What stands out most is Brieane's leadership philosophy: She reminds us that when companies are rooted in their values and evolve with intention, they don't just sell products—they build communities and create lasting impact."

—Artemis Patrick

President and CEO, Sephora North America

"I know firsthand that collaborating with your community is the secret to building something truly iconic. *Co-Created* is Brie Olson's love letter to culture and creativity—showing how listening and co-creation can transform not just a brand but the world around it. Community as the new couture! That's hot."

—Paris Hilton

CEO, 11:11 Media; Entrepreneur; Advocate; Celebrity

"Brieane Olson is the rare leader who blends vision with heart. In *Co-Created,* she shows how courage, community, and creativity can transform even the most legacy-bound brand into a cultural force. This book is a masterclass in transformation, but it is also a love letter to what's possible when vision meets resilience. Brieane's courage to challenge the legacy playbook, her relentless pursuit of relevance, and her ability to fuse creativity with operational excellence are the reasons Pacsun stands as a case study in reinvention. As a friend and client, I couldn't be more proud to stand beside Brieane as she shares this story with the world and to witness her redefining what female leadership looks like—bold, inclusive, and unapologetically authentic."

—Jennifer Prince

Chief Commercial Officer, Los Angeles Rams

"*Co-Created* is a definitive look at business transformation. Brieane Olson shows how Pacsun put community at the center to move forward with resilience, creativity, and leadership. It's a story of reinvention in a time when culture moves fast and expectations move faster. Every leader, in any industry, will find lessons worth carrying into their own work."

—Russell Wallach

Global President, Live Nation

"Turnarounds are challenging, each in their own way. Yet in Olson's hands, Pacsun's turnaround is a joyous re-creation that results in a new answer to the most fundamental of questions: Why is this business relevant? Her strategy was forged not in isolation but in co-creation, through authentic engagement with customers, purpose-led leadership, and an open and collaborative culture. Olson will convince you that it is all a deeply human endeavor. Get inspired by what she and her team did at Pacsun—then imagine what you could achieve."

—Cynthia A. Montgomery

Charles B. (Tex) Thorton Chair, Advanced Management Program, Harvard Business School

"Brieane Olson offers a powerful road map for revitalizing heritage brands by turning customers into collaborators. *Co-Created* proves that purpose, cultural fluency, and community engagement can drive sustainable growth and keep retailers ahead in a rapidly evolving market."

—Jill S. Dvorak

Senior Vice President, National Retail Federation

"*Co-Created* is such an inspiring and insightful look at how culture, creativity, and community can truly transform a brand. Brie's leadership shines through every page. She shows what it means to listen deeply, to build with purpose, and to lead boldly in a constantly evolving landscape. This book isn't just about Pacsun's reinvention; it's a playbook for any leader who wants to create meaningful impact by putting people and values at the center. I have such admiration for Brie as a leader, and I couldn't be more excited to celebrate this important work."

—Jennifer DiPasquale

President and Co-Founder, Women in Retail

"Brieane Olson understands what so many leaders still miss: Creators aren't just collaborators, they're co-architects of culture. In *Co-Created*, she shows how Pacsun has embraced co-creation not as a marketing tactic, but as a true business strategy—inviting creators and communities to help shape everything from products to storytelling. As someone who lives at the intersection of brands and creators, I've seen firsthand how Brie's vision has redefined what authentic collaboration looks like, and why Pacsun is now a cultural force that moves at the speed of its community."

—Chris Detert

Co-Founder and Chief Communications Officer, Influential

"*Co-Created* captures Brie's brilliance as a leader who sees what others can't. With vision, creativity, and a deep understanding of culture, she reimagined Pacsun's future while inspiring teams to build with heart and purpose. This book isn't just about brand transformation—it's a powerful blueprint for how Brie's unique blend of cultural insight and bold leadership can drive lasting growth."

—Melissa Campanelli

Co-Founder, Women In Retail Leadership Circle

"It is a privilege to discuss Brieane Olson and her new book, *Co-Created*, which highlights her vital contributions and vision for Pacsun's evolution in recent years. Today, the company represents far more than a retail brand; it stands as a cultural interpreter and leader within the industry, thanks to its thoughtfully curated designs and innovative marketing strategies.

Throughout her career, Brieane has been an invaluable friend, business partner, mentor, and source of inspiration across both creative and business sectors. As a prominent female leader in the fashion industry, she not only supports emerging designers but also champions established brands, delivering an empowering message to a new generation of young girls and future industry leaders. Her authentic insights into the intersection of fashion and contemporary culture underscore her strengths, grounded in integrity and a nuanced understanding of today's landscape. I consider myself fortunate to be part of her circle and wish her ongoing love, success, and happiness as she navigates her journey."

—Jeff Hamilton

Legendary Jacket Designer

"Pacsun gave me one of my first opportunities as a creator; seeing my casual fit check in my room turn into something way more impactful was incredibly surreal. It showed me firsthand how forward-thinking companies like Pacsun can empower creators to spark change. *Co-Created* beautifully captures that exact spirit of listening, connecting, and collaboration."

—Lyla Biggs

Creator

"I have worked closely with Brie for fourteen years and have witnessed her leadership skills up close. It is one thing to have a (co)create strategy in mind (which is brilliant, by the way), but it is another matter entirely to have the leadership skills to bring it to life. Brie and her team have done an exemplary job of infusing the (co)create vision throughout the organization and rallying all of Pacsun's (co)creators to collaborate and propel the Pacsun brand forward. In this book, Brie does a terrific job, not only describing the vision of customer-centric (co)creation but also spelling out a road map that every reader can follow to make it a reality. At Golden Gate Capital, we are delighted to have been along for this tremendous ride and are grateful to be partners with Brie and her team."

—Neale Attenborough

Managing Director, Golden Gate Capital

"I have had the distinct pleasure of working in partnership with Brie over the past fourteen years at Pacsun. Brie is a rare talent whose leadership inspires all around her—from the talented employees at Pacsun to the many creative and collaborative relationships with partner brands, co-creators, and suppliers. I am excited that Brie has put pen to paper to share Pacsun's incredible journey. *Co-Created* is a 'must-read' for any leader aspiring to create an enduring connection with their customers."

—Mike Montgomery

Managing Director, Golden Gate Capital

"Brie Olson was a classmate with whom I shared both joys and hardships at Harvard Business School's AMP, and we were the only participants from the fashion industry. In November 2024, during the collaboration between WILDSIDE—Yohji Yamamoto Inc.'s new project focused on partnerships—and Pacsun, launched at ComplexCon Las Vegas, she proposed a market-conscious branding strategy, welcoming Formula 1 to attract new fan bases. Her business strategy—consistently prioritizing a market-in perspective, including the element of 'good surprise,' while remaining trend-conscious—stems, I believe, from her profound insight and overflowing passion for the market. I look forward to seeing her continue to spearhead Pacsun in bringing fresh energy to the fashion industry."

—Tsuyoshi Muraki

Chief Development Officer, Yohji Yamamoto

CO-
CREATED

BRIEANE OLSON, PACSUN CEO

CO-CREATED

THE CULTURAL STRATEGY THAT REDEFINED PACSUN

Forbes | Books

Published by Forbes Books, Charleston, South Carolina.
An imprint of Advantage Media Group.

Printed in the United States of America.

10 9 8 7 6 5 4 3 2 1

ISBN: 979-8-88750-807-8 (Hardcover)
ISBN: 979-8-88750-808-5 (eBook)
ISBN: 979-8-88750-809-2 (Audibook)

Library of Congress Control Number: 2026901170

01-26-2026 5:19

To Jim.

CONTENTS

PROLOGUE

ELEVEN THOUSAND ASTRIDS

BLACK FRIDAY IS notoriously intense for retailers. At Pacsun, we start planning for it a year in advance. Three months prior, the preparation intensifies. By the time the big weekend arrives, we are having hourly calls to track numbers with our digital and field teams, monitoring website, social, and brick-and-mortar sales. Those calls continue through the weekend. On Black Friday weekend in 2023, one name came up repeatedly on those calls: Astrid.

To clarify: Astrid is a jean. More specifically, the Astrid wash of Pacsun's Casey Low Rise Baggy Jean. And Astrid would become a case study in what happens when strategic community building, social commerce infrastructure, and authentic creator partnerships converge at precisely the right cultural moment.

In the days leading up to Black Friday 2023, creator Lyla Biggs, as part of Pacsun's TikTok open creator affiliate program, posted a video featuring the now-famous low-rise jeans. Lyla's video—candid and simple, shot in her bedroom at home—was shared to her five thousand followers. Those followers liked, commented, shared, and bought. The algorithm picked up on that excitement, views increased, and the brief clip went viral.

By Black Friday, Pacsun had already sold eleven thousand Astrids. From there, the brand would go on to sell another sixty thousand pairs of the jeans on TikTok alone, plus hundreds of thousands in stores across the country. By the end of the weekend, all of our digital inventory had sold through. Everyone wanted the viral TikTok jean.

What made this moment significant wasn't the sales numbers themselves, but what they represented: a validation of a strategic approach to brand transformation that could be replicated, not only by Pacsun but also by other companies. The Astrid phenomenon demonstrated how legacy brands can successfully evolve by becoming purpose-driven, shifting their culture to prioritize community and then bringing that community into the conversation and further empowering them through the creator economy.

This wasn't about one viral moment. It was about creating conditions for sustainable growth through genuine community engagement. For brands looking to connect with younger consumers, for investors seeking companies positioned for the future of retail, and for partners wanting to work with organizations that amplify their communities, the weekend demonstrated a clear blueprint that spoke to a scalable, strategic methodology: Listen first, build together, and let your community lead the way.

So, how did Pacsun manage to go from struggling legacy brand to cultural force? This book is my attempt to answer that question. Ultimately, the answer lies in our commitment to our purpose: Pacsun seeks to inspire the next generation of youth, building community at the intersection of fashion, music, art, and sport. This transformation wasn't just about what we left behind; it was about what we stepped confidently toward—a vision to inspire, innovate, co-create, and take action alongside the communities we serve.

That shift was much larger than TikTok or any other platform. It spoke to a fundamental revolution in how Pacsun engaged with and addressed its customers, a change that proved far greater than any single medium. That pivotal shift is what allows us to connect so profoundly with youth culture today.

In the pages to come, I'll detail not only what we did to get there but also how we had to rethink what it means to be relevant along the way. Because relevancy is a constantly evolving process. The consumer is always moving, which means the brand is always refining its strategy. And the work of achieving relevancy is never complete, as it requires staying in lockstep with the consumer. What follows is both our methodology and our road map forward.

A VIRAL MOMENT, BUT NO COINCIDENCE

As the CEO of Pacsun, a question I'm often asked is, "How did you transform the brand?" The answer isn't simple, because it wasn't any one person who transformed Pacsun from an uncertain legacy brand to one that's now helping to shape current cultural conversations. It took the hard work of many talented and dedicated people at Pacsun and a community of creators, customers, and collaborators to help us reimagine what a youth culture brand could become. Just as no one person can claim credit for the shift, there isn't a single pivotal moment that marks the turning point. It's been a deliberate build, day after day, driven by strategic decisions balanced with calculated risks, all guided by one fundamental change: inviting our community to co-create the brand with us rather than dictating to them from the inside out.

That evolution is best understood through the moments when strategy, preparation, and community converged. One of those moments came on Black Friday, 2023. While this particular weekend would become emblematic of our co-creation strategy in action, it represented the culmination of years of thoughtful preparation. What happened that weekend wasn't luck; it was the result of listening to our community and positioning ourselves to amplify their voices when the moment was right.

There's a lot of history leading up to that viral moment in 2023, both for Pacsun the brand and for myself as the CEO. First founded in 1980 under the name Pacific Sunwear of California, the Anaheim-based company officially rebranded as Pacsun in 1999,[1] almost a full decade before I joined. In 2007, I came on board as the senior product line manager for men's and women's non-apparel (accessories and footwear).

By the time I joined, Pacsun was already fighting for relevance. The brand had been challenged by a number of macro issues, including the decline of shopping malls, the rise of fast fashion, and shifting consumer preferences away from traditional surf-and-skate culture. I'll discuss these in greater detail in the first chapter. However, the biggest issue of all was that Pacsun had failed to carve out a distinct identity for itself. We had never developed an authentic, original vision for the brand as we know it today, which is driven by a mission to inspire the next generation of youth and build community at the intersection of fashion, music, art, and sport.

---

1 Leslie Earnest, "Pacific Sunwear Now 'Pacsun,'" *Los Angeles Times*, December 29, 1999, https://www.latimes.com/archives/la-xpm-1999-dec-29-fi-48478-story.html.

Those issues culminated in Pacsun's Chapter 11 bankruptcy filing in 2016, a clear indicator that change was needed.[2] What we'd been doing hadn't been working. The question then became, What should we be doing differently? It took careful planning, strategic risk-taking, and the hard work of many people to formulate the answer. The most pivotal shift was that Pacsun became a brand of its own, co-created with consumers through thoughtful community engagement that positioned those consumers not as passive recipients of our messaging but as partners in our brand development. Pacsun may have been created in 1980, but it would take an iterative act of co-creation to revive it decades later.

Reimagining Brand and Product Through the Eyes of Customers

Fifteen years ago, Pacsun was a surf-and-skate destination in the American shopping mall, a store selling other brands and none of its own namesake. Now, roughly 50 percent of the products in Pacsun stores carry the Pacsun label. As for the other brands we carry, there have been changes there, too. As surf-and-skate brands such as Quik silver, Roxy, and Volcom have lost popularity and other brands have gained ground, we've followed suit, bringing in new brands such as Kendall & Kylie, Brandy Melville, and Fear of God Essentials. While we have great respect and admiration for surf and skate and its influence on Pacsun's founding culture, our strategy prioritizes customer relevance above legacy brand associations. Consumer

2 Thomas S. Onder, "Pacsun Files for Chapter 11 Protection in Delaware—Next Batch of Expected Retail Chapter 11 Bankruptcy Filings," *The National Law Review*, April 7, 2016, https://natlawreview.com/article/Pacsun-files-chapter-11-protection-delaware-next-batch-expected-retail-chapter-11.

relevance is fundamental to retail viability, and sustainable retail operations depend on product–market alignment.

As we navigated this transformation, we developed a comprehensive approach to customer feedback, listening to our consumers at every decision point. We didn't just listen; we actively invited dialogue. What did they like? What did they hate? What did they want to see in stores, online, and on social media? What made them connect with Pacsun, not as a retailer but as a brand? And how could we build that brand, together with them, to create something that went beyond clothing—to develop a community?

That strategic reimagining of our brand, our product offering, and our creator relationships created the foundation for what happened on Black Friday 2023. We created the conditions for that viral moment in other ways as well. We had established our presence on TikTok in 2019, recognizing its potential beyond what others saw as a "dance app," and built a following of two million engaged users in roughly eighteen months. The platform became a channel for demonstrating Pacsun's authenticity and cultural relevance while advancing our evolution into a purpose-driven brand. While we contributed content, our growing community increasingly drove the narrative. Generations Z and Alpha began creating content on our behalf, and we intentionally encouraged this shift. This marked our formal entry into co-creation, an extension of our traditional approach to social media and commerce that invited the everyday consumer to speak for our brand.

By November 2023, we had cultivated a substantial community of co-creators on TikTok while simultaneously building the technical infrastructure needed to support social commerce. When we initially joined TikTok, there was no TikTok Shop, the e-commerce platform that is integrated within the app today, allowing users to discover and purchase products directly through the platform. However, we had anticipated this development, so when TikTok Shop launched in September 2023, our technical team was ready to implement the necessary infrastructure.

While external observers might have attributed the Astrid success to viral luck, our internal team knew it was the outcome of deliberate planning. The jean's viral moment was the result of strategic preparation across multiple fronts: our evolution into a purpose-driven organization that prioritizes community collaboration, product development aligned with consumer values, and a marketing strategy that amplifies rather than dictates.

Although we had been building toward Black Friday 2023 for years, that weekend surprised us in some ways, providing new insights that would help fine-tune Pacsun's strategy from that point forward. We hadn't anticipated that Pacsun's viral moment would come from TikTok's open creator platform specifically. To clarify, TikTok has two creator pathways: the regular TikTok platform, where anyone can post videos, and TikTok's open creator platform, which is a more structured program that connects brands directly with vetted creators to develop sponsored content and partnerships. The open creator platform provides creators with campaign briefs, performance metrics, and guaranteed compensation, while regular TikTok relies on organic discovery and its algorithm.

We also didn't anticipate the halo effect of Astrid's viral moment. The cross-channel impact exceeded our projections. Beyond TikTok sales, we observed increased foot traffic in physical stores, with customers specifically requesting "the TikTok Jean," a testament to the omnichannel impact that social e-commerce can have. It was also noteworthy to us that this impact was generated by a micro creator. In the increasingly egalitarian modern media landscape, even a micro creator (defined as a creator with fewer than ten thousand followers) could make a big impact.

Additionally, we gained a new appreciation for how this model could empower individuals within the creator economy. Lyla Biggs earned compensation through her Astrid campaign on the open creator platform, while Pacsun benefited from authentic community advocacy. This mutual enrichment exemplifies the collaborative approach that defines a modern, purpose-driven brand: You must build with your customers. Successful brands are no longer created from the inside out. They're built collaboratively.

Validating Our Thesis: Co-Creation as a Competitive Strategy

Ultimately, Black Friday 2023 affirmed our theory that sustainable brands must create ecosystems rather than transactions, building purpose-driven communities where customers feel genuinely connected to something meaningful beyond the product itself. It's not just about a low-rise jean. There are plenty of competitors who could produce a low-rise jean. The competitive advantage lies in authentic community engagement and consumer investment in the brand's purpose, identity, and values.

November 2023 was a data point showing us the power of co-creation. We took that data and adjusted our approach accordingly. Before Astrid, we had been investing less than half of our marketing/advertising resources in the open creator platform, with more money going to more traditional media (such as paid ads on TikTok). Today, the breakdown is almost the exact inverse, with substantial resources going to open creator platforms.

The shift toward co-creation and creator-first commerce has gone hand in hand with a move toward greater inclusivity. While we once focused on targeted collaborations, we now welcome more far-reaching partnerships. Instead of Pacsun contracting ten individual creators on socials to talk about the brand—us choosing them—people choose *us*. Creators who are interested in supporting the brand can reach out to us, and we'll send them a sample pair of jeans, but there's no contract tied to it. Now that TikTok has become a social commerce giant, accounting for almost 10 percent of total e-commerce business in 2024 alone, those creator relationships can prove very fruitful, not only for us but also for the members of our community, such as Lyla Biggs.

It's an intriguing shift. Prior to digital, opportunities for consumer control were limited. People were told what was cool to wear by fashion magazines, and products were sold through six-figure ads featuring top models. There was little opportunity for dialogue. A person could show what they liked by where they spent their dollars and, maybe, by participating in the occasional consumer survey over the phone or by mail.

Today's retail landscape demands genuine dialogue between consumers and brands. While many companies fear losing narrative control, Pacsun's embrace of platforms such as TikTok's open creator platform represents the logical evolution of our purpose-driven approach: We invite anyone who connects with Pacsun to become part of our community and help shape our future.

The foundation of this strategy is systematic social listening across multiple platforms and real-time response to consumer signals. Following this approach, our teams have been able to identify future trends years before the mainstream adopts them, and we're now developing AI-driven algorithms to enhance our ability to anticipate and respond to cultural shifts. This comprehensive listening approach, from social media engagement to merchandising decisions, enables us to make strategic bets based on data rather than intuition alone.

PURPOSE AS FOUNDATION: DEVELOPING AUTHENTIC CONSUMER RELATIONSHIPS

Authentic engagement with youth culture requires sustained commitment and consistent action that aligns with stated values. Today's consumers expect brands to demonstrate genuine commitment to their principles through measurable initiatives. This means translating values into operational decisions. At Pacsun, we don't just *say* we stand for diversity and inclusion; we practice that through our actions and words, from when we speak up about social causes to what we carry in stores (for example, we stock more than 15 percent minority-owned brands).

The traditional retail approach of avoiding social discourse is no longer viable when consumers actively seek purpose-driven brand leadership. Today, 82 percent of shoppers say a brand's values need to match their own, and 39 percent say a value mismatch would be grounds for them to permanently boycott their favorite brand.[3] Those findings aren't exclusive to the United States but have been seen at a global scale.[4] And Gen Z in particular is leading the charge, with 50 percent prioritizing buying from socially responsible companies.[5] This generational shift toward values-based purchasing represents

3 Giusy Bounfantino, "New Research Shows Consumers More Interested in Brands' Values than Ever," *Consumer Goods Technology*, April 27, 2022, https://consumer-goods.com/new-research-shows-consumers-more-interested-brands-values-ever.

4 "People Prefer Brands with Aligned Corporate Purpose and Values," *World Economic Forum*, December 17, 2021, https://www.weforum.org/stories/2021/12/people-prefer-brands-with-aligned-corporate-purpose-and-values/.

5 Kieran Smith, "Marketers Courting Gen Z Aim to Hit the Right Notes," *Financial Times*, June 17, 2025, https://www.ft.com/content/c3709f51-c28b-4530-b1c2-af108c0fa260.

a fundamental change in consumer behavior that extends beyond fashion retail. Authenticity is in demand, now more than ever.

Whether it's in our conversations with consumers or in the choice of people we partner with, authenticity guides us at every step. When A$AP Rocky joined Pacsun as a guest artistic director, he told the story about the nostalgia he felt for the brand and how he wanted to bring it to all kids and make it accessible because he remembered shopping in a Pacsun store as a kid and what it had meant to him. That's the kind of real, tangible connection we look for with the people we partner with, and that purpose-led authenticity has guided Pacsun's transformation—a transformation rooted in co-creation.

That spirit of co-creation has led to impactful dialogue, not only with our consumers but also with the brands and people we partner with creatively, from Formula 1 racing to The Metropolitan Museum of Art to Japanese fashion designer Yohji Yamamoto. In line with our purpose-driven culture, we also seek partnerships with impact. Our work with Rare DNM and Selena Gomez, giving back to her mental health foundation, exemplifies this approach. We're no longer just partnering with a celebrity to have them tell a story on our behalf. We are doing it because it's someone who aligns with our values and who is likewise deeply connected to the community. Further, we actually put our money where our mouth is—every transaction gives back, demonstrating how fashion can be a force for positive change.

As we've embarked on such initiatives, we've increasingly found ourselves not just participating in the current cultural conversation but helping to define it. This positions us for long-term sustainability in an increasingly volatile climate, where everything from tariffs to new media can have an impact. It's less about the platforms we use and more about the community we've built, because that community is what will stand the test of time.

Whether our community is found on TikTok or moves to other platforms, we will continue to evolve with it, letting the community members lead the way. Who knows what technology will arise in the next five, ten, or twenty years. In the future, TikTok may not be the same source of connection with our community that it is today. However, there's no denying that it's played an important part in our past journey—and that journey began long before Black Friday 2023, in an unexpected setting that would come to symbolize our willingness to take strategic risks: in the Sahara Desert.

CHAPTER 1

STILL SELLING CALIFORNIA

IN EARLY 2020, ten members of the Pacsun team, myself included, headed to Morocco for a photoshoot for the 2020 back-to-school campaign, featuring the company's latest denim line. Designed, produced, and branded by Pacsun, the denim product was one component of a larger strategy shift away from serving as a "house of brands" that only carried other retail names to defining the company's own original brand. This denim campaign celebrated more than product creation. It was part of our thoughtful evolution from retailer to co-created brand.

The Morocco shoot took place in the desert outside Marrakech, an intentional choice of location. With its rich, warm hues, the environment harkened back to the California sunshine while representing the reach we wanted Pacsun to have across the globe. For the shoot, we brought twelve content creators with us to model the looks, most of whom had significant followings on Instagram, the social media platform of the moment. But these creators weren't just models—they were cultural intelligence partners whose insights would help inform our community-led brand strategy.

After a long afternoon of shooting in the desert sun, we spent the evening around a fire. The days were sweltering, but when the sun set, a chill would descend on the pink sands that had us clustering around the warmth of the flames. With no Wi-Fi and spotty cell service cutting us off from the digital world, we found ourselves in rare, uninterrupted conversation. The creators we'd brought, young voices who understood youth culture in ways traditional focus groups never could, started sharing what they were seeing in their communities. What platforms were gaining traction? Which brands felt authentic versus performative? How was Gen Z actually shopping and expressing themselves? At the time, I was the chief merchandising officer, so I was constantly seeking these kinds of unfiltered insights, and here they were emerging organically in the Moroccan desert.

The conversation that evening centered on a strategic question we'd been analyzing for months: How should Pacsun make its entry onto TikTok? Our decision to join the platform was the result of dedicated research into emerging platform-building opportunities. TikTok was still a relatively new phenomenon in the US, known primarily as a digital space where young people posted videos of themselves dancing to short clips of music. Although the platform was not yet set up for e-commerce, we expected it would evolve in that direction, so we had decided to establish a presence early. Our research had also indicated that TikTok users were trending younger compared to platforms such as Facebook and Instagram. And those users were the ones buying Pacsun. This aligned with our broader strategic thesis:

Sustainable growth required meeting our community where they were actively engaging, not where traditional retail expected them to be.

Although the data confirmed that our gut instinct to get on TikTok was the right thing to do, that did not answer the question, What should our first post be? Our TikTok strategy exemplified our shift toward community-first marketing: Rather than creating content about youth culture, we would invite young voices to co-create our brand narrative. We had identified a TikTok trend that used a "cute jeans" soundbite, which aligned well with our current denim campaign. We'd already done enough research into TikTok to know that trends were fleeting. If we wanted to use the opportunity, we had to move fast. So, rather than waiting until we got back to California, we decided to leverage that moment and share our first TikTok from Morocco.

The next morning, we approached Mathieu Simoneau, one of the creators on the trip with us, and asked him if he'd be willing to be featured in our post. He was hesitant at first. Like many creators in early 2020, he still saw TikTok as just a dance platform. Nonetheless, he agreed. So, before the Morocco trip concluded, we created and uploaded Pacsun's first video to TikTok, featuring Mathieu. The brand had been confidently stepping toward a more globalized, less SoCal-specific image for years. This, the first TikTok filmed far away from Pacsun's California roots, was another thoughtful step in that progression.

ANCHORED BY A LEGACY: EARLY SIGNS OF DISCONNECT

That first TikTok post did not go viral. It did not make headlines. It did not smash any records in terms of likes or comments or follower gains. And it did not result in any direct sales, as TikTok Shop would not launch for another few years. While the post generated modest initial engagement, it established a foundation for our long-term social commerce strategy, opening new avenues for engaging with our core audience and, later, e-commerce opportunities. Meanwhile, for Mathieu, it accelerated his career trajectory. Today, he has more than one million TikTok followers and is a brand ambassador for Louis Vuitton. This mutual success validated our approach to community-led content creation.

The fact that Pacsun's first TikTok was posted from the bustling hub of Marrakech, a world away from the brand's roots in Southern California, is significant to me. Although we didn't plan it that way, it was yet another step in shifting Pacsun from the SoCal surf-and-skate brand it had once been to a more globalized, diverse brand that met consumers where they were at, embracing their many different lifestyles rather than limiting them to just one.

Pacsun has a very powerful brand legacy. While that can be a good thing, it can prove damaging if that legacy keeps the brand from moving with the currents of change. In its infancy, Pacsun created a strong identity inspired by the quintessential SoCal lifestyle. It was built on polished imagery of beautiful beaches and surf scenes. I was born and raised in San Diego, and to me, vintage Pacsun represents Huntington Beach, a seaside city in Orange County that features almost ten miles of sandy beach and is known for its ideal surfing conditions and strong beach culture.

The brand's roots made sense in the early 2000s, when brands such as Volcom, Quiksilver, and Roxy were in high demand—those brands were doing amazing business, as was Pacsun. Surf and skate entering mainstream fashion was a big moment, and Pacsun was at the forefront of it. This led to a surge of store openings, a type of nonstrategic growth that would prove impossible to sustain as the popularity of surf and skate faded from the mainstream. As we entered the mid-2010s, Pacsun found itself still trying to sell the SoCal surf-and-skate lifestyle at a time when our consumers were looking for something else. Even as we started to look beyond surf-and-skate brands, we often found ourselves pigeonholed by consumers who still associated us with this realm, especially older consumers, such as Millennials and Gen X, who remembered us from our days as a shopping mall destination.

This raises another important macro factor that was dragging Pacsun down: Malls were not doing well. In the mid-2000s, a boom in mall construction led to an oversaturated market, and many malls faced increasing competition, struggling to attract shoppers. Oversupply created an unsustainable market structure, with the 2008–2009 recession accelerating the closure of anchor stores such as JCPenney and Sears and fundamentally altering consumer shopping patterns.[6]

Another macro factor at play was the rise of e-commerce. Pacsun was losing market share to the many up-and-coming online retailers flooding the market, including fast fashion retailers. E-commerce and fast fashion represented more than competitive pressure; they signaled a structural shift in consumer expectations around price, convenience, and speed to market. While our commitment to ethical manufacturing prevented direct price competition, we were competing for the same consumer dollars, and that pressure was felt.

The visibly shifting cultural climate was another indicator that Pacsun was not just falling behind but falling out of touch with the consumer. Our market analyses revealed a generational disconnect: Gen Z prioritized inclusivity and multi-identity expression, while our

6 Karen Meier, "The Growth, Decline, and Rebirth of the American Shopping Mall: Part 1," Camoin Associates, October 10, 2023, https://camoinassociates.com/resources/the-american-shopping-mall-part-1/.

product mix remained anchored to binary surf-and-skate aesthetics that no longer resonated with emerging youth culture. The old Pacsun still prioritized surf and skate, which often operated on a strict binary: bikinis for girls, board shorts and skateboarding shoes for boys. This was complicated by the fact that our product offering skewed heavily toward male shoppers. I'd estimate that when I joined the business in 2007, the ratio of men's to women's fashion was about 70:30. Given that US households spend nearly 62 percent more on women's apparel than men's apparel, that ratio alone presented a challenge.[7]

Significant strategic effort was required not only to avoid being seen as just a surf-and-skate brand but also to avoid being seen as a guys' store that excluded female shoppers. In an attempt to address both points, we began to diversify and carry other brands, such as Kendall & Kylie and Brandy Melville. At the same time, we were clinging to our heritage of surf and skate, so we ended up blurring the lines of what we offered, still without developing a clear brand of our own. We were trying to be everything to everyone, and in the process, we never defined who we were. Amidst that complexity, most consumers fell back to their preconceived notions of Pacsun as a surf-and-skate brand. Moreover, market data confirmed that mainstream consumers were losing their affinity for those brands and, with it, losing their affinity for Pacsun. Weighed down by its SoCal legacy, Pacsun was unable to transform that public perception.

These were not isolated challenges. They represented fundamental shifts that required systematic transformation rather than incremental adjustments. The first signs of disconnect, already visible to anyone paying attention, quickly trickled down to the bottom line. Well before the company filed for Chapter 11 bankruptcy, the hard

---

7 U.S. Bureau of Labor Statistics, "Apparel Data in Fashion," *The Economics Daily*, February 5, 2025, https://www.bls.gov/opub/ted/2025/apparel-data-in-fashion.htm.

numbers foretold that outcome. Store teams started reporting slower consumer response to the core styles and brands that had once been Pacsun's bread and butter. Store performance deteriorated, sale comps slowed, and revenue decreased. The performance data confirmed earlier assessments: A sweeping transformation was needed.

STUCK BETWEEN PRODUCT AND CULTURE

A comparison of Pacsun stores in 2007 versus 2025 illustrates the scope of our brand transformation. In a 2007 Pacsun store, clothing was clearly divided into designated sections according to gender norms: board shorts on one side of the store and women's swimwear on the other. The racks mostly held surf-and-skate brands, such as Roxy, Quiksilver, Volcom, and etnies. There was not a single item in the store with a Pacsun label.

A modern Pacsun store paints a very different picture. Take the Pacsun SoHo flagship store in New York City as an example. The SoHo store debuted a new look in 2022, after being decorated with Pacsun's Etoile Monogram Capsule pattern. The capsule collection was designed to be completely gender-fluid, and the campaign for it featured Mathieu Simoneau as well as TikTok star Emma Chamberlain. The SoHo store doesn't have surfboards or skate ramps, and it's been redesigned so that the fashions aren't male- or female-oriented but all-encompassing, creating a harmonious space where people don't feel limited by gender-specific sorting. Brands that used to dominate the racks, such as Roxy, Quiksilver, or Volcom, are nonexistent, while newer brands have taken their place, from edikted to Formula 1 to Fear of God Essentials. And about half the apparel in the store carries the Pacsun label, including everything from graphic tees to denim and accessories.

A clothing label might not seem like a big deal. But for a retail brand, it's significant. Think of a teenager's closet. If they're asked to pull out their favorite pair of jeans, they can probably do so in an instant and immediately provide a brand identifier: "Oh, I love these Levi's!" or "I love my Rare DNM jeans!" It doesn't matter if they bought those jeans at Pacsun, or even if Pacsun designed them, as was sometimes the case when we would create a product but not actually label it Pacsun. The recognition is in the brand. This is why Pacsun's shift is so significant. Now, there are teenagers who pull out their favorite sweatshirt and tell the world, "This is my cozy Pacsun sweatshirt!" or who make a social media post in their denim and proudly proclaim, "I love my Pacsun jeans!" Creating someone's favorite piece of clothing is the first step to creating lasting brand love. That's why it's so significant that modern Pacsun stores carry Pacsun-branded products, not just other brands. This shift from retailer to brand creator fundamentally changed our value proposition and relationship with our customers.

Internally, there was a quiet knowing that we were headed down a precarious path. However, there was not yet a coordinated response. Although we were doing some interesting things, it wasn't enough to impactfully change our trajectory, and many of our efforts were reactive rather than strategic. For example, in an effort to get business back up, we'd look at what was working for other brands, say, Abercrombie or Urban Outfitters, and then try to emulate them. Scrambling to rebound, we were simultaneously chasing trends while also trying to elevate the brands we already carried, and without a distinct brand identity, we failed on both counts. Without the strength of our own brand foundation, we couldn't create a compelling reason for customers to choose Pacsun over our competitors.

In short: We lacked clarity. Clarity about what our consumers wanted, clarity about how to move forward, and most significantly, clarity about what we stood for as a brand. A brand is much more than a label on a pair of jeans. It also represents a culture, a community, a way of viewing and engaging with the world. And Pacsun simply hadn't developed any of that. It had basically hooked into surf-and-skate culture when it was popular with consumers, and as that waned from the mainstream, it struggled to define what was next.

Stuck between product and culture, we ended up not standing for enough. And for younger generations seeking purpose-driven brands rooted in authentic community and values alignment, that was a losing proposition, which meant it was also a losing proposition for Pacsun.

WHEN HERITAGE BECOMES A BARRIER

In the fashion world, there are trends and fads, and then there are consumer shifts. A fad disappears when trends shift. But a true market shift reshapes how consumers think, behave, and buy across categories. By the time I joined Pacsun in 2007, it was evident that the company was not aligned with what the up-and-coming Gen Z actually cared about: identity, values, co-creation, digital expression … But the issue was bigger than that. It wasn't just that there had been a change in consumer taste. Various macro factors, from the rise of social media to the decline of shopping malls, were resulting in a larger consumer shift. And amidst that shift, Pacsun was in danger of being left behind.

At a time when Pacsun should have been rapidly evolving to keep up with the transforming retail culture and consumer base, it remained stuck, moving too slowly and clinging too adamantly to its heritage. Instead of looking to the future, the brand looked largely to the past. Agreements with old brands that were no longer selling were maintained for longer than they should have been. Stores were kept in locations that were no longer profitable. For too long, instead of inviting consumers to co-create the brand with us, we simply tried to build the brand from the inside out.

The leadership team had to confront a difficult truth: Their emotional attachment to Pacsun's surf-and-skate heritage was becoming a barrier to progress and no longer serving the current customer base. The transformation required recognizing that being co-created in Los Angeles meant something bigger than surf and skate—it meant embracing the entrepreneurial spirit, creative innovation, and inclusive energy that define California culture. This wasn't about rejecting our past but about continuously refining the unique processes that drive our business to serve a broader, more diverse community, united by shared values of creativity, inclusion, and positive change.

Still, the tension between honoring roots and staying relevant created a painful dilemma. True reinvention required acknowledging that while the company's surf-and-skate origins deserved respect and gratitude, staying relevant to constantly aging-out consumers meant being willing to evolve. This transformation would require not only internal but also external change—and ultimately, a change in leadership, because even with internal advocates, true transformation requires absolute buy-in from the top.

By the time I joined Pacsun, the rumblings of change were already underway. Within weeks of joining the company, I was brought onto the Mavericks project, an eighteen-month transformation initiative that would become a cautionary tale about the perils of trying to be everything to everyone. While born from genuine recognition that change was necessary, Mavericks would ultimately illustrate one of the most common pitfalls in corporate transformation: the temptation to layer superficial changes over existing structures rather than fundamentally rethinking what the brand might become. The project's struggles would reveal why half measures in transformation efforts often fail, setting the stage for the more radical reimagining that would eventually follow.

CHAPTER 2

NOT QUITE MAVERICK

IN 2007, I LEFT Abercrombie & Fitch and joined Pacsun as the director of men's and women's non-apparel. Within weeks of my joining, the company launched Project Mavericks, a transformation initiative meant to help Pacsun rediscover its relevance. I was new to the team and had not anticipated having a role in so concretely helping shape the company's future. Although unexpected, the opportunity to be part of the conversation about Pacsun's next steps was highly inspiring, indicating a chance to enact real change. The only problem? Enacting real change is harder in practice than it is in theory.

The eighteen-month transformation initiative brought together the executive team, a carefully selected group of individuals from within the company—a cross section of people at different levels throughout the organization—and external consultants specializing in everything from creative to strategy. My role within the team focused largely on bridging the gap between merchandising and design.

I think everyone taking part in the project, the people known as Team Mavericks, tried very intently to get the best possible outcome and bring the initiative to life in a meaningful way. Our goal? Try to modernize while preserving the company's core identity. That would prove to be an almost impossible balance to strike. Still, at the start, there was a great sense of optimism, fueled by the recognition that change was desperately needed and the genuine belief that the effort could spark true change.

The urgency was real, as the business was struggling significantly. Among other things, the Project Mavericks team was tasked with answering the following questions:[8]

- What's the best strategy for driving value at Pacsun, now and in the future?
- What should the Pacsun brand stand for?
- What kinds of unique customer experiences can we create?
- What must we strengthen in our people, processes, and tools?

Knowing there were no magic answers, we chose to make the work a collective process of discovery, informed by simple ground rules:[9]

- **See:** Be open to taking a different look.
- **Believe:** Be active in reshaping your opinions and beliefs.
- **Think:** Work with all the brains in the room to think boldly.
- **Act:** Focus on where real value is created.

The high-level outcomes of Team Mavericks' work were summarized in a sixty-plus-page book, entitled simply *Mavericks*. The final pages were a call to action, a summary of how the spirit of the project could

8 *Mavericks Pacsun 2007* (Stone Yamashita Partners, 2007), report provided to Pacific Sunwear, Inc.

9 Ibid.

be kept alive going forward: "Here's how we can keep the spirit of Mavericks alive. Keep exploring. Keep collaborating. Keep leading. Keep going."

Despite the ambitious sign-off, the project was not able to save Pacsun from having to file for Chapter 11 bankruptcy less than a decade later. While Project Mavericks *did* accomplish a lot of great things, planting seeds for more effective transformation that would come later, it ultimately floundered.

WHAT PROJECT MAVERICKS ACCOMPLISHED

Project Mavericks concluded by identifying eight big shifts the company needed to commit to in order to help transform its brand. I am providing those here to help demonstrate how the strategic framework for transformation was, in many ways, already in place. What was missing was the organizational commitment and dedicated execution needed to bring these principles to life. Also missing were the values that would define our later transformation: integrity, passion, innovation, and teamwork. While the project recognized the need for customer centricity, it hadn't yet embraced the co-creation model that would become central to our purpose-driven approach post-bankruptcy.

Nonetheless, as you read these principles, you'll likely see the early seeds of some of the fundamental shifts I outlined in the prologue and first chapter of this book. These are the eight principles of Project Mavericks, as outlined in 2007:[10]

10 Ibid.

1. The customer will be central to everything we do. Youth culture is created by teens, not adults, and we need to live and breathe their culture.

2. Pacsun will be more than the name on the door. We'll make it a covetable brand. In the past, we've viewed ourselves as a retailer. Now we'll build up Pacsun as a brand that makes other brands cool.

3. We'll consider the brand in every part of the business, every day. Brand thinking will guide big and small decisions, from whom to hire to how to run the supply chain.

4. We'll take our cues from style leaders. Our customers, and the customers we want, aspire to the confidence of style leaders. We believe we can make every teen feel like a style leader.

5. We'll offer a strong and unique point of view on fashion. We've always been in the fashion business—and emerging fashion is more than surf-and-skate apparel. We'll be the trusted editor for teens.

6. We have a great heritage based on surf and skate, the beach, and California, and now we'll take it further. No one has yet brought an updated take on Southern California life and style to the malls of America, one that reflects the street as well as the beach.

7. We'll shift time, resources, and energy to the most effective work, not just the most efficient. From a customer-focused supply chain to the right tools and technologies, we'll transform our people and operational capabilities to support ambitious brand and growth goals.

8. We'll inspire the rest of Pacsun with our vision for change. The Mavericks team can lead the way for an overall culture change, through the work we do and through the way we do it.

Looking at those eight principles, certain phrases jump out at me, hinting at concepts that reflect later changes. "The customer will be central to everything we do" is an ethos Pacsun upholds to this day. The language about making Pacsun a "covetable brand" rather than a retailer reflects the shift to actually having Pacsun-labeled clothes, which I discussed in the previous chapter. The nod to taking "cues from style leaders" reflects Pacsun's subsequent work with celebrity tastemakers of the era, such as Kendall Jenner and Kylie Jenner. Finally, in more than one of the principles listed above, there was a tacit acknowledgement that the brand needed to expand beyond surf and skate—for example, "emerging fashion is more than surf-and-skate apparel" and "an updated take on Southern California life … that reflects the street as well as the beach."

These broader principles were supported by more granular strategic initiatives, from building our trend-spotting skills to reinventing the Pacsun customer experience. Looking at these principles now and knowing that they were supported by thoughtfully developed tactical shifts, it seems that Project Mavericks was on the right track. But less than ten years later, the company would file for bankruptcy. So, what went wrong? Why was Project Mavericks not the turnaround moment we had hoped it would be?

Ultimately, I think you can look to the name itself to identify the core issue: A maverick is defined as an independent individual, someone who does not go along with a group or a party. While I can appreciate the upside of that message, the desire for Pacsun to confidently establish itself as a unique, relevant, and covetable brand among consumers—a trendsetter rather than a trend follower—that spirit of hyper-independence is very much at odds with the spirit of co-creation we embrace as a brand today.

This tension between independence and collaboration would manifest throughout the initiative. While we wanted to be mavericks in the market, recognized as bold, innovative, and trendsetting, we were approaching transformation as individual actors rather than as a unified team working with our community. True brand transformation, as we would later learn, requires the opposite of maverick behavior. It requires thoughtful collaboration, both internally among teams and externally with consumers. The most successful brands aren't mavericks operating in isolation; they're community builders that understand that sustainable relevance comes from authentic partnership rather than top-down innovation.

That drive for independence was reflected in many of the issues that would hold back Project Mavericks from realizing its full potential, including a siloed internal culture and a lack of authentic listening to consumers at all levels.

LESSONS LEARNED FROM PROJECT MAVERICKS

Project Mavericks got a lot of things right. It also got some things wrong. Looking back on the initiative now, more than a decade later, a few lessons learned stand out to me. I wouldn't characterize these as missteps or mistakes but more as underrealized efforts, underscored by insufficient support, a lack of strategic alignment, underutilized resources, and a general inability to follow through.

The fundamental issue was that we focused on changing our thinking without changing our actions in a cohesive, collaborative, well-thought-out way. We were not yet in lockstep internally, and this made it impossible to get into lockstep with our consumers. This fundamental principle applies not just to retail transformation but to any organization seeking to build authentic relationships with its community. Broadly speaking, the below learnings speak to four essential components of organizational change: leadership foundation, internal culture, external relationships, and execution and commitment.

Leadership Foundation: Effective Change Requires Absolute Buy-In from the Top

First, it's important to note that Project Mavericks was largely driven by outside consultants. Consultants can be incredibly useful, and I believe those who supported Project Mavericks did excellent work, providing actionable takeaways, recommendations, and insights into consumer behavior and emerging market trends. However, being outside the organization, they could play little to no role in implementation. And for actual implementation to happen, there needs to be buy-in from the top. In Pacsun's case, this buy-in was impeded by pivotal changes in leadership.

Project Mavericks was initiated under an interim CEO. Later, a CEO who had not been part of the transformation initiative was hired to replace this interim figure. Incoming executives often have their own playbook, as they want to do things their way rather than executing someone else's vision. For those of us who had been on Team Mavericks, there was a real dichotomy about what we had identified as a promising path forward versus what we were supposed to do under this new leadership. But we adapted and moved forward under the new direction. Unfortunately, the strategic continuity got lost in the transition.

Added to that, many of the internal people who had been part of Team Mavericks were let go after the new CEO's arrival, leaving behind only a small group of us to try to push the project's agenda forward. Many of us remaining advocates didn't have an executive presence at the time. Since we were more junior in our careers, it became difficult to drive change, especially without full leadership support.

This was seen in internal decision-making processes, for instance, in assortment meetings. In retail, this is where teams decide which products to carry in stores and online, curating the assortment or product mix for the coming seasons. Someone more junior would propose a new idea—say, a denim style such as the jegging—and suggest we start it small because the customer wasn't ready for it yet. Then a senior decision-maker would get overzealous about the idea and insist on making it a huge initiative, operating from an antiquated view of marketing where the brand tells the customer what they want rather than taking the time to understand authentic trend development. The company would then buy way too much inventory of this new idea that hadn't really been customer-tested, the product wouldn't sell, we'd have to mark it down, and our margins would suffer as a result.

Looking back, this was a case study of what not to do if you want to build a truly consumer-centric brand, and very much at odds with one of the stated principles of Project Mavericks: "Youth culture is created by teens, not adults, and we need to live and breathe their culture." However, with new leadership having its own agenda and not fully championing the principles of Mavericks, it proved difficult to forge ahead on the path the initiative had set out.

LESSON LEARNED: Today, we adopt a "test and learn"—or "read and react"—strategy at Pacsun. Leadership trusts teams to implement this framework in decision-making, empowering them to act independently, with full support from leadership assumed. We've found that sustainable change requires both internal cultural alignment and external community validation working in tandem. The most effective strategies emerge when leadership teams are authentically committed to co-creation rather than dictation and when that commitment translates into consistent action and organizational ownership.

Internal Culture: You Can't Build an Authentic External Community Without Internal Alignment

Transformation efforts don't just require absolute buy-in from the top; they also require comprehensive culture change within. This was impeded by the fact that Pacsun was still a very siloed organization at the time of Project Mavericks. For example, there remained a disconnect between product and design versus marketing, as the product evolution itself was not matched by the marketing transformation or a clear brand position. Without cohesive marketing support, even successful product initiatives couldn't reach their full potential or create the unified brand experience that would truly connect with consumers.

This fractured approach was informed by a fundamental values misalignment. If you look at the company's internal values back in 2007, they were focused on individual excellence and implied rivalry rather than collaboration. Individuals and teams were often competing with one another within the company's four walls, rather than banding together to move change initiatives forward. When you're trying to build an external culture focused on community-building and togetherness, having that kind of internal culture is inherently going to undermine those efforts.

Since then, our values have evolved significantly, emphasizing teamwork and a purpose-driven approach. One of the cornerstones of our current culture is, "We work together to win. We listen to one another, reaching consensus and supporting group decisions. We celebrate achievements. We respect and trust one another and commit to our company goals, leading to our success as a team." This is further echoed by our brand promise, which includes the statement, "We win as a team."[11]

This internal values shift has been paralleled by structural changes, as our offices evolved from closed spaces to an open floor plan, breaking down the literal barriers that contributed to internal silos and smoothing the path toward more seamless collaboration. We also made adjustments to tangibles such as bonus structures, shifting from a discretionary individual bonus model to team-based bonuses that any employee (not just an executive) is eligible for.

LESSON LEARNED: A real internal culture shift comes from people feeling trusted and like they can be honest with one another. This creates the kind of camaraderie and community that we want to reflect outside. It only makes sense that if we are going to embrace a culture of co-creation *beyond* the company's four walls, that same spirit must also be found *within* the company's four walls.

External Relationships: True Consumer Centricity Requires Genuine Collaboration

Project Mavericks recognized the need to put the customer at the center of everything Pacsun did. It's in that first principle: "The customer will be central to everything we do." In that spirit, Pacsun did introduce initiatives to get to know our customers better. However, even as we leaned into consumer research, we didn't fully implement the results

11 "Who We Are," Pacsun, accessed June 20, 2025, https://www.Pacsun.com/company/about.html.

of that research in a way that reflected consumers' wishes, instead continuing to try to dictate change from the inside out.

One step in the right direction was the creation of our Style Leader program. These were actual consumers who were selected, handpicked from our stores and even our competitors' stores, to provide real-world insights into the brand. We basically invited them to tell us what we were doing wrong. We might ask them questions like:

- What were the last three pairs of jeans you bought? Why did you buy them?
- What's on your wish list? What are things you're looking for right now?
- What stores do you shop at most frequently? What do you buy there? Why?

The resulting two-way discussions marked a pivotal shift, as we came to see these conversations as an essential tool for understanding our customers by letting them lead. We had realized that we could not tell them what was cool; they had to tell us what was cool. However, while we were bringing consumer voices into our process, we were still ultimately trying to control the conversation in many ways.

For example, after hosting a one-way mirror focus group to hear from customers, we would then organize those customers into distinct buckets: "He's a surf guy. She's a Brandy girl. He's an athlete. She's a skater who's also into streetwear." This ignored a general consumer shift toward greater fluidity. Youth fashion was moving beyond singular identities and toward a more malleable form of self-expression. The same teenager might dress in streetwear one day and in a frilly skirt and tank the next. However, we were still building product around very specific, one-dimensional customer profiles, trying to lead the consumer to the product rather than letting them lead us.

This inside-out approach was fundamentally at odds with today's model, where we operate in lockstep with behavioral changes. The concept of *style leaders* is also no longer applicable. Back then, the idea was that style leaders (the most forward, trend-focused consumers) would adopt new fashions first, and then it would trickle down to the masses at a slower speed with time. This model no longer works in the same way. Today, everyone has social media, which gives them access to trends instantly through their phones. As a result, trends now happen at the same clip globally rather than filtering down from a small group of very stylish early adopters.

LESSON LEARNED: Even as we listened more closely to customers post-Mavericks, we were still approaching consumer insights as information to be gathered rather than relationships to be built. We would collect feedback, analyze it, and then decide how to use it, rather than creating ongoing dialogue where consumers could actively participate in shaping the brand alongside us. True consumer centricity, as we've since learned, requires moving beyond research sessions and focus groups and toward authentic community engagement, where the conversation never stops and the consumer becomes a genuine collaborator rather than a subject to be studied. This distinction would prove crucial in our later transformation: the difference between listening *to* consumers and listening *with* them as partners in co-creating culture.

Execution and Commitment: Evolution Can't Be Accomplished with Half Measures and Hesitation

Project Mavericks was an incredible accomplishment, and I do not want to discount the hard work and effort of the many people who made it possible. In terms of strategic vision, it set Pacsun on the right path in many ways. It was just the implementation of that vision that faltered, for the various reasons listed above. Further, I'd suggest that Project Mavericks failed largely because it did not go far enough, as we were still holding on to our past and insisting on marketing that heritage identity *to* the consumer, rather than creating with them. Hesitation resulted in half measures that could only change the brand but not truly transform it.

Additionally, many of the changes implemented were superficial rather than fundamentally shifting the needle. Branding changes were implemented; for example, the logo was modernized, and many, though not all, retail locations were modernized. With such updates, the brand may have ended up looking more current, but it was not actually more connected.

This was also reflected in the products we continued to carry. A hesitation to fully commit to transformation meant that promising initiatives often remained underutilized rather than becoming the foundation for broader change. We would bring in new brands, which was the right thing to do. However, internal debates about moving too far from Pacsun's surf-and-skate heritage carried on. While we did have some product evolution and genuine steps forward (for example, bringing in brands such as Kendall & Kylie in 2013), it often felt like we were taking one step forward and two steps back.

Part of this was due to the fact that there were critical constraints holding us back from moving forward. Old brand relationships are one example, as we had signed contracts requiring us to design product on behalf of various brands and to purchase minimum quantities of those brands. If we bought less than those contracted amounts, those brands wouldn't sell to us anymore. So, teams were forced to focus on maintaining those brand relationships rather than making decisions based on consumer insights.

When new, popular brands appeared alongside brands that weren't appealing to the current consumer base, there was a disconnect. For instance, our sales analytics showed virtually no cross-shopping between new brands such as Brandy Melville and legacy surf brands. A consumer would come in to buy a Brandy item and only buy that; they weren't necessarily tempted by the Roxy board shorts on the hanger nearby. We were essentially operating multiple disjointed boutiques under one roof rather than creating a cohesive brand experience that encouraged broader exploration and deeper engagement with the Pacsun identity.

LESSON LEARNED: Following Project Mavericks, there was significant internal debate about how big we wanted these new initiatives to be. The resulting trepidation created a pattern where we would make a change but then pull back and wait to see the results of that change before allowing ourselves to catapult forward again. The brand still lacked a clear identity and purpose, and while there were some positive product changes, there wasn't a fundamental transformation. Now we know that singular changes alone aren't enough to reposition a brand. A clear purpose is needed.

CULTURAL SHIFTS OUTPACING CORPORATE CHANGE

I do not want to undermine the importance of Project Mavericks. In fact, I would say the project itself was a success. It acknowledged that we needed to evolve. That assessment was correct, and many of the fundamental shifts the project sought to implement reflected that. The board at the time also acknowledged the magnitude of the moment. The Mavericks book that summarizes the change initiative has a quote from one board member stating, "I have goosebumps on my goosebumps. This work is great."[12]

Thanks to Project Mavericks, we did accomplish some important things in the years that followed: listening more thoughtfully to our consumers, modernizing our branding and retail spaces, and establishing impactful strategic partnerships with everyone from Kendall and Kylie Jenner to the incomparable Virgil Abloh. Virgil would go on to push boundaries as the artistic director of Louis Vuitton menswear and the founder of Off-White, transforming the fashion industry by proving that streetwear belonged in the world of high fashion. His loss in 2021, at just forty-one years of age, left a hole in the creative world. We were fortunate enough to work with him, and his creativity, generosity to emerging voices, and belief that fashion should be accessible and inclusive continue to inspire what we do today.

Despite these new partnerships, efforts at change were still impeded in many ways: by a lack of leadership buy-in, siloed ways of working, evolving brand relationships, and a continued failure to engage in meaningful dialogue with consumers that went beyond "What do you want to see on the racks in our stores?" And while we *said* the consumer was part of all decision-making, and we took steps toward that, we weren't truly in lockstep with our customers. There was collaboration but not yet the authentic co-creation that would define our later success.

Although Project Mavericks planted the seeds of change in 2007, it lacked the targeted implementation needed to really see those

---

12 Stone Yamashita Partners, *Mavericks Pacsun 2007.*

changes take hold in a lasting, meaningful way. And in the decade that followed, Pacsun would face new challenges. During this period, significant cultural shifts were occurring that would reshape retail entirely. Hip-hop and rap music created huge cultural momentum, and streetwear evolved to gain relevance at every level of fashion. Icons such as A$AP Rocky and Travis Scott represented new style influences. Gender-fluid style was emerging. And fast fashion retailers such as Forever 21, Nasty Gal, and Fashion Nova were bringing new trends to market more swiftly than traditional retail calendars could accommodate, creating additional pressure.

At the same time, social media was beginning to create a more globalized fashion influence. You no longer had to travel to Japan to get a glimpse of Tokyo street style, for example; you just had to pick up your phone and start scrolling. The accessibility to fashion that social media allowed also chipped away at the idea of style leaders or icons. Anyone could become an influencer, and trends could emerge from anywhere. A teenager's bedroom in Ohio was just as likely to spark a viral fashion moment as a runway in Paris.

Pacsun's preexisting problems came into sharper focus. Despite moments of progress, Project Mavericks had stalled. Without full organizational commitment and leadership continuity, we continued working in silos rather than driving toward our shared vision. This resulted in a partial execution that would ultimately prove insufficient for the scale of transformation that was needed. Ultimately, Project Mavericks would not be able to keep the company from filing for Chapter 11 bankruptcy, a pivotal moment that made it clear: Now, a *real* change was needed.

CHAPTER 3

REALITY HITS HARD

ON APRIL 7, 2016, Pacsun filed for Chapter 11 bankruptcy protection in the state of Delaware. A bankruptcy sounds like it should be a huge dramatic event, a crisis that inspires fear and panic. The reality, as I experienced it from inside the company, was quite different.

Leadership at that time had done a good job—some might argue too good a job—of insulating us against the realities of Pacsun's money troubles. There was an almost overbearing air of optimism in the months and weeks leading up to the filing. Even though our public stock was trading at a dollar prior to the filing, a sign that something was very wrong, leadership was still acting like everything was fine. Not just fine, but great. With that attitude at the helm, there was perhaps a false sense of security internally. As a result, the bankruptcy announcement took many of us on the inside by surprise. Still, there was no sense of panic around it generally across the company.

Even after the filing was announced, the messaging around it was positive: It was presented as a simple, logical business decision, not as a last-ditch effort to save the company. In some ways, that is exactly what it was. Used appropriately, bankruptcy can be a useful tool to help a company get back on its feet. Pacsun is a testament to that, and I'll detail how the company made use of this decision to restructure, financially and organizationally, with an eye toward sustainable success. Still, it felt like leadership was presenting the situation as just a blip when, in fact, it was a major shake-up.

On top of the business repercussions, there were also the reputational implications to consider. The media covered the news with varying degrees of nuance. Here is a sampling from the time:

- **"Pacsun Files for Chapter 11 Bankruptcy Protection, Plans to Go Private"—*Los Angeles Times*:** "On Thursday, the Anaheim apparel company commonly known as Pacsun filed for Chapter 11 bankruptcy protection, the latest in a string of California teen activewear retailers that have struggled to adapt to changing fashion trends. Those companies have been plagued by the same issues facing many apparel companies—the move toward online shopping instead of bricks-and-mortar stores, and the popularity of so-called fast fashion retailers, which quickly cycle through new looks and stay up-to-date with the latest styles."[13]
- **"The Long, Agonizing Fall of Pacsun"—*Bloomberg*:** "Once a staple merchant of California cool, Pacsun wasn't able to adapt as fashion trends left surfwear behind and overexpansion sapped its resources. It amassed crippling debt as it recorded

13 Samantha Masunaga, "Pacsun Files for Chapter 11 Bankruptcy Protection, Plans to Go Private," *Los Angeles Times*, April 7, 2016, https://www.latimes.com/business/la-fi-Pacsun-bankruptcy-20160407-story.html.

losses each year since 2008. Every effort at reinvention failed. Executives couldn't figure out how to stop the bleeding."[14]

- **"Where Did It All Go Wrong for Pacsun?"—*GQ*:** "Two days ago, reports circulated indicating Pacific Sunwear, better known as PacSun, is set to file for Chapter 11 bankruptcy. With that news, the retailer's stocks plummeted—they currently sit at just 10 cents per share. (This time a year ago, they were around $2.50.) The question here, of course, is what happened? From the late '90s to the mid-aughts, PacSun was pretty much *the* one-stop shop for teens to get the latest skate- and surf-inspired gear. By stocking mass-market outdoor brands like Billabong, Quiksilver, and Burton, it dressed an entire generation of kids in California-cool vibes. But in more recent years, the brand seemed to be repositioning itself as a streetwear haven. [...] But the news of the bankruptcy means that its repositioning was either too late or too difficult to actually pull off in such a large operation ..."[15]

The varying perspectives highlighted the complexity of Pacsun's situation. While *Bloomberg* focused on our financial struggles and repeated failed reinvention attempts, *GQ* recognized our strategic pivot toward streetwear but questioned our execution speed or capability. The *LA Times* positioned us within broader industry trends affecting teen retailers. Each perspective contained elements of truth without accurately articulating the full picture. We had struggled with debt and overexpansion, we were indeed repositioning toward

---

14 Kim Bhasin, "The Long, Agonizing Fall of Pacsun," *Bloomberg*, April 8, 2016, https://www.bloomberg.com/news/articles/2016-04-08/the-long-agonizing-fall-of-pacsun?embedded-checkout=true.

15 Jake Woolf, "Where Did It All Go Wrong for Pacsun? (Update)," *GQ*, April 7, 2016, https://www.gq.com/story/pacsun-bankrupt-chapter-11-why.

streetwear, and we were part of a larger retail disruption. However, none of the media coverage captured the full strategic context of what we were building toward. Nonetheless, these media narratives would become part of our story, reinforcing the need for clearer brand communication and more focused transformation efforts.

While the business and fashion media did report on the Chapter 11 filing, we were fortunate in that there was overall very little mainstream coverage about it, and I think very few of our customers actually ended up hearing about it. We kept an eye on socials to see if the news was trickling down from the business media to more popular platforms, and there was barely any mention of it. However, retail professionals and investors heard the news, and I'm still asked about it to this day, even though I was not CEO at the time, instead holding the position of senior VP of merchandising and design.

Even now, almost a decade later, the Chapter 11 filing remains part of Pacsun's story in business circles. I was teaching at Columbia University in the spring of 2025, and one of the students asked what it was like to take the company through Chapter 11. The Chapter 11 filing has thus become a permanent part of Pacsun's story, requiring ongoing explanation and context, which I hope to provide with this chapter. Although I did not step into the CEO role until 2023, more than seven years after the bankruptcy filing, I have a unique vantage point on both the necessity of that restructuring and the thoughtful approach to transformation it ultimately enabled.

BANKRUPTCY 101: THE LOGISTICS OF CHAPTER 11

Pacsun's Chapter 11 filing was a prepackaged bankruptcy. This means that the company had a plan for financial reorganization, prepared in cooperation with its creditors, before it formally filed. The goal of such an approach is to save on expenses and reduce turmoil. While I was not responsible for the business decisions that informed the decision to file or how it was subsequently handled, I recognize that the process was efficient and effective. Pacsun has even come to be recognized as a brand that bounced back from bankruptcy and has been cited as a case study that others can learn from.

From an article entitled "Here's How Three Bankrupt Retailers Bounced Back, and What Debt-Ridden Brands Can Learn from Them" by *The Business of Business*: "PacSun worked with Golden Gate Capital and Wells Fargo to reorganize through a debt-for-equity agreement … With restructuring, PacSun 'transitioned beyond its historical roots' according to Josh Olshansky, a Golden Gate Capital managing director, and brought in additional brands to create a more well-rounded offering representing 'California style.'" [16]

While the bankruptcy was happening, these big-picture changes were not immediately felt. For my part, I was immersed in the day-to-day tasks required to maintain operations. Now, looking back, I am able to take a more analytical view, recognizing the core components that allowed for Pacsun to leverage the bankruptcy as a positive instigator for change rather than a crippling indicator of ruin: financial restructuring, store/lease restructuring, operational continuity, and stability in leadership.

Financial Restructuring

Pacsun's intentional approach to financial restructuring was one reason that the bankruptcy didn't incite the panic it might have otherwise.

---

16 Jessica Hicks, "Here's How Three Bankrupt Retailers Bounced Back, and What Debt-Ridden Brands Can Learn from Them," *The Business of Business*, September 2, 2020, https://www.businessofbusiness.com/articles/bankrupt-retailers-coronavirus-data-american-apparel/.

Another reason was that Pacsun was already familiar with the firm that was acquiring the company to take it private—Golden Gate Capital had been an investor since 2011, initially as a minority partner, but, with the bankruptcy, it planned to become a majority partner.[17] The firm demonstrated a strong belief in Pacsun's ability to turn things around and backed up that belief with both actions and words.

Golden Gate Capital converted more than 65 percent of Pacsun's term loan debt into equity and provided a minimum of $20 million in additional capital to support the company's long-term growth objectives.[18] The financial restructuring was accomplished in only five months, as Pacsun filed in April 2016 and emerged from bankruptcy in September 2016, a relatively short timeline.[19] For many businesses, one and a half to five years is a more reasonable timeline to complete this process.[20]

Golden Gate Capital issued the following statement at the time: "Pacsun offers consumers the most compelling and desirable mix of brands celebrating the California lifestyle. Now, with a strengthened balance sheet, reduced long-term debt and reduced annual occupancy costs, the company is well-positioned to build a stronger future and achieve long-term success. We look forward to continuing to partner

17 "Pacsun," Golden Gate Capital, accessed June 20, 2025, https://goldengatecap.com/company/Pacsun/.

18 "Golden Gate Capital Acquires Pacsun," *Private Equity Wire*, September 9, 2016, https://www.privateequitywire.co.uk/golden-gate-capital-acquires-Pacsun/.

19 "Golden Gate Capital Acquires Pacsun; Pacsun Emerges from Chapter 11 Restructuring with $20 Million in Additional Capital," Golden Gate Capital, September 12, 2016, https://goldengatecap.com/golden-gate-capital-acquires-Pacsun-Pacsun-emerges-from-chapter-11-restructuring-with-20-million-in-additional-capital/.

20 "How Long Is the Chapter 11 Bankruptcy Process?," Kerkman & Dunn, accessed June 20, 2025, https://kerkmandunn.com/how-long-is-the-chapter-11-bankruptcy-process.

with Pacsun and its experienced management team as the company executes its strategic plan …"[21]

When Neale Attenborough, managing director of Golden Gate Capital, addressed Pacsun employees on the day of the bankruptcy filing, he posed the following question: "Is today a good day or a bad day for Pacsun?" His point of view was very clear: It was a good day—because Golden Gate Capital believed in Pacsun's future growth and understood that this financial restructuring was what we as a company needed at the time to unlock our full potential as both a brand and a retailer.

Although I was not heading up Pacsun then, I am nonetheless deeply appreciative of Golden Gate Capital for their belief in the brand. Private equity firms often get criticized, but I found Golden Gate to be very intelligent, genuinely curious about the business, and committed to our future. They had a clear view of both the brand's challenges and its potential for growth. And as the people coming in and technically taking over, they helped to put into place a strategic plan that demonstrated a genuine understanding of what Pacsun needed to become.

LESSON LEARNED: The quality of your financial partners can determine whether a crisis becomes an opportunity for genuine evolution or not. Golden Gate's combination of industry knowledge, strategic mindset, and genuine curiosity about the business created the foundation for the transformation that would follow. True partnership means investing in what a company can become, not just solving what went wrong.

---

21 *Private Equity Wire*, "Golden Gate Capital Acquires Pacsun."

Store/Lease Restructuring

Pacsun's store fleet was another factor influencing financial performance that required restructuring. By 2016, Pacsun had grown to over nine hundred stores across the country. Many of these stores were located in what retail industry professionals call B- or C-malls, while today, Pacsun's stores are primarily located in A-malls—an evolution I'll touch on further in chapter 7. The A-B-C classification is used in real estate to assess the quality performance and investment value of a shopping mall. The ratings are based on factors such as sales performance (the dollar amount generated per square foot), tenant mix, location, and occupancy. For example, an A-mall may generate $1,000 in sales per square foot and have a high proportion of premium brands, such as Apple and Whole Foods, while a B-mall may generate something like $500 per square foot and have a high proportion of brands like H&M and Bath & Body Works.

Pacsun's founders and early management had driven growth largely through new store openings rather than same-store sales growth. As a result, the company had signed a number of expensive ten-year-plus leases, often above the market rate. Many of these locations simply weren't strategically thought out; they were opened just to generate growth instead of as part of a thoughtful market penetration plan.

Added to that, as the institution of the American shopping mall faced its own struggles, foot traffic in these spaces waned, and Pacsun's narrow SoCal surf-and-skate positioning could not generate demand among the shoppers who were still seeking out brick-and-mortar retail. The company was over-penetrated in terms of store fleet relative to actual market demand. The Chapter 11 filing addressed this by reducing that fleet, allowing the company to get out of the most expensive, underperforming leases and reducing annual occupancy costs significantly.[22]

Today, Pacsun operates about 310 stores and has plans to grow to a maximum of 450, following a more thoughtful approach that considers market needs, not just a desire to grow. E-commerce has also taken a larger chunk of business, growing from some 10 percent in 2016 to approximately 40 percent today, making the need for brick-and-mortar spaces less pressing for the time being.

LESSON LEARNED: Looking back, the store fleet restructuring was essential not just for financial reasons but because it forced us to think more strategically about where and how we connect with our community. The shift toward digital engagement has allowed us to maintain that connection while operating a more sustainable physical footprint, a better foundation for the co-creation model that would define our later success.

Operational Continuity

While the bankruptcy announcement didn't create a sense of panic, it did require some damage control, especially with our vendors. With Golden Gate Capital's support, all of Pacsun's branded partners, both large and small, were paid in full.[23] This commitment to honoring contracts was critical in helping ensure operational continuity in both the present and the future. Part of my role at the time was to help communicate this to our vendors while also providing some more general reassurance as to Pacsun's future.

---

22 Golden Gate Capital, "Golden Gate Capital Acquires Pacsun."

23 Ibid.

With this goal in mind, I joined the then-CEO on a road show to visit our key brand partners. We talked to them about the restructuring, how it would be a quick and clean transaction, and explained how beneficial it would be in the long term, not only to Pacsun but also to Pacsun's partners. We were basically selling the future story of Pacsun with the goal of making sure our brand partners would keep shipping to us. We'd already received our funding from Golden Gate Capital at this point, so we could confidently share that vision.

The approach was direct and transparent, driven by clear communication. As I recall, the message was straightforward: This is just what we need to do to position Pacsun for long-term success. We were able to persuade and convince our brand partners that they should believe in what we were doing enough to stick with us, and those conversations became signs of advocacy and understanding—a recognition that sometimes public companies go private for the right strategic reasons.

Looking back, I think that my focus on the task at hand insulated me against the financial realities of what the company was going through and prevented some sense of panic. If I had been in a different role (say, as a VP of finance), I would likely have a very different recollection of this time. But I was somewhat protected in the more creative product world, focused on building the future of Pacsun and trying to stay in that space of imagining what our future state could become.

LESSON LEARNED: Authentic stakeholder communication during crisis requires genuine belief in your future vision, backed by concrete commitments. The road show succeeded not because we minimized the challenges but because we had established extremely strong brand and vendor relationships—and could demonstrate financial stability through Golden Gate's support and a strong belief in Pacsun's future.

With that said, exactly what that future looked like was still unclear. The bankruptcy was an undeniable red flag that it was time for a real transformation, not a transformation of hesitancy and half steps. However, the question remained whether we would finally have the organizational alignment necessary to execute a total transformation in practice.

Stability in Leadership

The restructuring essentially allowed Pacsun to shed expensive leases, reduce its debt burden, and gain financial stability while maintaining operations and relationships. That is not to say that it was an easy road. Emerging from bankruptcy brought its own challenges. Pacsun had endured its moment of reckoning. The question was, What now?

That question became complicated by an abrupt change in leadership. Less than a year after the bankruptcy concluded, the CEO was exited and an interim CEO was put in their place. James Gulmi came from outside the organization, and the team at Pacsun was not familiar with him. But any trepidation we had around this interim figure was quickly laid to rest. Jim was a former CFO who had worked with a managing director at Golden Gate Capital decades earlier. In his previous role, he had been the longest-standing CFO of that public company. Although he had since retired, he came out of retirement specifically to help Pacsun through its transition.

Jim, as our interim CEO, brought the financial acumen and diligence that Pacsun needed at that time. His approach was practical and direct, basically summed up by "You cannot lose money, and you have to make sure you don't run out of cash." His background was exactly what the organization needed. He also became a mentor to me personally, indirectly helping me prepare to step into the CEO role myself down the line.

The bankruptcy itself was relatively quick and clean, and the leadership shake-up that followed, although unexpected, proved critical to Pacsun's subsequent transformation. The interim CEO's financial grounding created a foundation that allowed creative initiatives to flourish without the financial chaos that had previously undermined transformation efforts. Now, with financial stability preserved, Pacsun could turn its attention to the fundamental brand issues that remained largely unaddressed.

LESSON LEARNED: Sustainable transformation requires both creative vision and operational discipline working in tandem. Previous efforts had often emphasized one at the expense of the other, either pursuing creative initiatives without financial rigor or focusing so heavily on cost cutting that innovation suffered. Under stable leadership that understood both the creative potential and the operational requirements of brand building, Pacsun finally had the platform needed for authentic transformation.

BEYOND BANKRUPTCY: TIME FOR A REAL TRANSFORMATION

The bankruptcy had erased any last doubts that such an authentic transformation was needed. The optimism that had been the go-to of previous leadership gave way to an authentic assessment. It soon became clear that many of the problems first identified by Team Mavericks more than a decade earlier were still there, having been only partially addressed and never fully solved. Mavericks was right about a lot of things; it's just that those things weren't as fully embraced and implemented as they needed to be.

There were still internal issues to overcome. The organization continued to operate in a very siloed fashion. Men's and women's departments were treated distinctly, despite the fact that consumers were interested in more gender-fluid fashions. The lack of alignment between men's and women's was reflected in some glaring differences. For example, while the women's fashion we had been carrying trended younger, say, tweens and teens, the men's fashion we'd been carrying had trended older, say, mid- to late-twenties. In this way, internal dichotomies were directly impacting our consumers and their retail experience.

Another issue identified by Team Mavericks but never solved: Pacsun was still seen largely as a retailer, a carrier of other brands, rather than as a brand itself. We did design products, but we weren't putting our name on them. There was a denim line called Bullhead, for example, that was designed by Pacsun, but because it had a Bullhead label on it rather than a Pacsun label, nobody actually knew it was by Pacsun. If you had asked a teenage girl about her jeans, she'd simply tell you, "They're Bullhead!" No mention of Pacsun.

This all added up to the challenging truth I articulated in the book's introduction: Pacsun lacked a clear brand position. We were still trying to be everything to everyone without articulating what *we* stood for. The bankruptcy gave Pacsun permission to thoughtfully figure out what that identity and, with it, the brand's future, might look like. Part of that meant cutting out what hadn't been working, but part of it also meant looking at what *had* been working.

In the years leading up to the bankruptcy, there had been success stories. We'd seen lines around the block when we held store events for the Kendall & Kylie brand, for example, and when Rita Ora came to our Santa Monica store to promote her collaboration with adidas. These events helped us understand the power of partnerships that created something unique and special—something that was only found at Pacsun and was endorsed by influential voices.

We had also developed partnerships with designers such as Virgil Abloh, Jerry Lorenzo, Matthew Williams, and Heron Preston. This work positioned us authentically in streetwear and demonstrated what was possible when we focused on cultural relevancy at the intersection of music, fashion, and influence. Whether through the Jenners and their Hollywood and fashion influence or through streetwear partnerships that connected to broader cultural movements, we were getting strong consumer feedback that suggested a clear direction forward.

I should note that this was at a time when celebrity partnerships were the dominant path for cultural relevance. Back then, people were looking to major celebrities for style direction. It was different from today, when community influence and peers at a teen's own school can be more influential than how celebrities dress. Although Pacsun broadened beyond celebrity collaborations toward a more inclusive spirit of co-creation, these partnerships created authentic excitement at the time and hinted at the power of co-creation to come. The challenge was taking these isolated successes and turning them into a cohesive approach to brand building.

FROM FINANCIAL RESET TO BRAND RESET: BUILDING ON WHAT ACTUALLY WORKED

The bankruptcy had given us something invaluable: permission to stop protecting what wasn't working and start building what could work. For the first time in years, we had financial stability, operational clarity, and leadership alignment pointing in the same direction. The bankruptcy reset created space for a brand reset rooted in our emerging purpose. We began to understand that being co-created in Los Angeles meant something bigger than any single aesthetic. It meant embracing the entrepreneurial spirit, creative collaboration, and inclusive energy that define authentic California culture. The foundation was set for the true transformation that would define Pacsun's future—one built on authentic community engagement rather than internal assumptions about what customers wanted.

Getting in alignment with the consumer requires being honest with yourself about where consumer sentiment lies. And that isn't necessarily gleaned from traditional feedback forums. Pacsun's success stories prior to the bankruptcy, the moments that had hinted at cultural relevance potential, reflected a mindset evolution, a move from being less about heritage preservation to more about consumer connection. Instead of being driven by traditional market research, these moments were shaped by social listening and real-time consumer feedback.

The Style Leaders program we'd implemented as part of Project Mavericks was one example of this, one of those moments that showed we *had* been on the right track in some ways. We had these young kids, lifted straight out of Pacsun's stores, telling us what was and wasn't cool. Today, that kind of unfiltered feedback is easily available online, where brands can have honest conversations with their customers. Initiatives such as Style Leaders were the first hints of our current co-creation strategy, a direct invitation to our customers to step into our community and help shape our story.

Our celebrity collaborations were also a step in this direction. No, they were not a co-creation model, as we were still dictating what style the consumer would want through our work with these partners rather than putting the community at the center of our partnerships. However, these initiatives showed a fundamental understanding of the need to listen to the cultural conversations our customers were already having, rather than trying to create those conversations for them.

In short, the celebrity partnerships taught us that authentic engagement required moving beyond one-way brand communication and toward genuine community dialogue—a lesson that would prove essential for the road ahead.

As Pacsun emerged from bankruptcy, those of us on the inside reflected on the company's previous success stories to help figure out the best path forward. Clearly, a change was needed, but good work had been done in the years prior to the filing. The question became: How could we build on what was already working?

CHAPTER 4

THE JENNER EFFECT

ONE OF THE most noteworthy success stories from the years preceding the bankruptcy filing was Pacsun's collaboration with Kendall Jenner and Kylie Jenner. The launch of the Kendall & Kylie clothing collection became one of those coveted moments when youth culture, fashion, and celebrity converged to create genuine excitement and authentic conversations among Pacsun's existing customers. It also brought in a lot of new customers.

We debuted the premier collection nationwide on February 8, 2013, kicking off with two in-store events, one in New York and another in New Jersey. The sisters—then in their teen years—attended in person, and the first three hundred participants were guaranteed a face-to-face meet and greet with them. Before the big day, excitement was bubbling up online. The posts performed well in terms of metrics such as likes, but to me, what was really interesting was the more qualitative feedback seen in the comments.

A January 29, 2013, Pacsun post teasing the line shows a picture of the sisters wearing the clothes, with Kendall in jeans and a tank and

Kylie in a skirt, tank, and bomber. The comments give you an idea of the eager sense of anticipation, not just for the event but for the sisters and the clothes themselves. User @danielle_malka wrote, "@pacsun feb. 8th!!!!!!!!! cant wait!!!!!!!!!!" while @kaitlin.wellborn commented "Love them!!!" and @denisemrtnz simply added "Jacket ❤❤."[24]

On the day of the launch event, the response was even bigger than we had anticipated: Tweens and teens lined up around the block, eagerly hoping for a chance not only to meet the sisters but to be among the first to shop their curated designs in person. That pattern repeated again and again, with young people flocking to Pacsun's Kendall & Kylie events across the country, from Chicago to California. A mall was forced to close during one of the events because of the onslaught of mall traffic driven by the sisters.

The excitement of those in-person gatherings carried over into the online sphere, which was gaining ground as *the* place to get fashion and style inspiration. Back then, young people were still looking primarily to celebrities for ideas on what to wear (today, they're more likely to look to their own peer groups), so the timing was perfect. We had strategically positioned ourselves at the intersection of cultural relevance and authentic partnership. At the time, Kendall and Kylie weren't yet the cultural icons they are today. The media still largely framed them as the little sisters of Kim Kardashian. However, their stars were clearly on the rise, and Pacsun was part of their advance in cultural relevance.

Here's a look at the YouTube comments on an interview featuring Kendall and Kylie as they launched their 2013 holiday collection at the Pacsun Store in Glendale, California. User @Racheldivaa wrote,

---

24 Pacsun (@pacsun), "The lovely @kendalljenner and @kyliejenner showing off a few pieces from their Kendall & Kylie Collection at today's shoot," Instagram post, January 29, 2013, https://www.instagram.com/pacsun/p/VC5DvxRpol/.

"They are the best ♥ i love them way tooo muchhhh," while @hazel5gh added, "they are literally so nice to their fans."[25]

And here are some comments on an Instagram post giving a behind-the-scenes look at the Jenners modeling their line at Saddlerock Ranch in Malibu. From user @aabcdfref: "cant wait! hopefully they sell small sizes like XS and 00 or 0(:" and from @christymeis, simply, "That's a pretty shot."[26]

Finally, take a look at the replies to Pacsun's July 22, 2016, post showing Kylie modeling a dress from the sisters' new Golden Child collection. User @caity.huxley commented, "This dress looks so nice @gigigye," while @seriously.skylarrr alerted their friend with, "@ taydenseay she is always slayin ()." Meanwhile, @makennalynnx just wrote, "@alayna_maee WANT" to which @alana.mhb replied, "Is this dress on the website?"[27]

Even a cursory overview of the comments gives you a good idea of how valuable the conversations we were starting to have with our consumers were. We were not only seeing enthusiasm for our collaboration partners and the brand but also getting real-time feedback related to the product. (See the request for specific sizes from @ aabcdfref and the question about a dress being available on the website from @alana.mhb.)

We were also seeing such interactions on Twitter, Snapchat, Facebook, and Pinterest—the digital spaces that young people

---

25 "Kendall Jenner and Kylie Jenner Launch Their 2013 Holiday Collection Exclusively at Pacsun," product launch in Glendale, CA, posted November 10, 2013, by WMTV, YouTube, 3 min, 59 sec, https://www.youtube.com/watch?v=gc40ds7xHiU.

26 Pacsun (@pacsun), "We captured this behind the scenes pic of @kendalljenner and Kylie @iputthedistrictonmyback on location at Saddlerock Ranch, CA," Instagram post, January 16, 2013, https://www.instagram.com/p/Uj1kgSRpqL/.

27 Pacsun (@pacsun), "Our girls @kendalljenner & @kyliejenner just launched their 'Golden Child' collection exclusively on pacsun.com!," Instagram post, July 22, 2016, https://www.instagram.com/p/BIJRGxVAQ1Y/.

were giving their attention to back then. Pacsun's own activity on these platforms was amplified by Kendall's and Kylie's social media profiles, which brought millions of followers into the conversation. The amplification effect was remarkable. On Instagram alone, Pacsun had approximately two million social media followers, while Kylie commanded eighty-five million. When a Jenner tagged Pacsun, the reach was exponential, and we saw our social channels growing with each collaborative post.

However, the real excitement wasn't the extended reach—it was the conversation that was starting to happen in our growing community. This wasn't a monologue, a brand trumpeting messages *at* its followers; it was a dialogue, and our community was getting involved in new and creative ways we hadn't anticipated. We saw online creators posting "Pacsun Haul" videos featuring the Kendall & Kylie brand, while others took campaign images and essentially cut their own promo videos for the collection. People weren't just responding; they were getting actively involved in their own creative moments.

As the collaboration continued, mainstream media picked up on the excitement, and we saw accelerated coverage there as well. From a 2016 *Teen Vogue* feature: "Kendall and Kylie Jenner make quite the design team. They're churning out every item in your closet from swimwear to handbags. But one of their first fashion ventures—their line with Pacsun—offers their best work yet, if you let them tell it. 'We've been working with Pacsun for so long now that we really wanted to top ourselves. This is our best work yet,' the sisters said in an exclusive statement."[28]

28 Jessica Andrews, "The Unexpected Styling Trick Kendall and Kylie Jenner Swear By," *Teen Vogue*, June 2, 2016, https://www.teenvogue.com/story/kendall-kylie-jenner-pacsun-ad-video.

Kendall and Kylie's fashion collaboration with Pacsun was initially an exclusive deal, so for three years, we were the only clothing and accessories brand they were pairing with. Eventually, they would go on to other ventures, establishing a partnership with Topshop and subsequently creating their own clothing line, as well as Kylie's cosmetics line. With time, their lifestyles evolved, and they focused their energy elsewhere.

Although the partnership may be in the past, being able to witness their evolution into the cultural icons they are today was incredibly rewarding. Over our decade-long relationship, we saw Kendall's transformation into a runway model working with luxury brands and Kylie's emergence as a beauty entrepreneur with her own empire. Our teams had the unique opportunity to work closely with them during their formative years, contributing to their growth while they contributed to ours. This mutual evolution reinforced our belief that the most valuable partnerships are those where both parties invest in each other's success over the long term, creating shared growth rather than transactional exchanges.

REAL PEOPLE, REAL PARTNERSHIPS, REAL IMPACT

Today, Kendall and Kylie are a sure bet. However, at the time when they started their collaboration with Pacsun, this wasn't yet clear. A lot of people saw them simply as figures from *Keeping Up with the Kardashians*, little more than kids who had grown up on reality TV. They hadn't yet established themselves in the fashion world. Nonetheless, noting the interest the Jenners generated among younger generations, Pacsun decided to take a bet on them. Looking back, we can say it paid off.

The success was largely due to the nature of the partnership—it was *real*. This wasn't a matter of the Jenners stamping their names on products they weren't involved in developing. I was VP of women's design when the relationship began, and in this role, I witnessed the Jenners' involvement firsthand. Regular visits to our Southern California offices became the norm, with Kendall and Kylie participating in twenty-person design meetings that included tech, design, fabric, and sourcing. They tried everything on themselves, were involved in fittings, and, despite their young age, demonstrated remarkable business acumen—they wanted to understand what was working across our broader business, not just in their line. This wasn't celebrity licensing; it was genuine collaboration. From concept meetings to trend discussions and campaign development, they were active partners in shaping everything from Coachella-worthy designs to their own swim line.

Kendall and Kylie were also active in the brand's promotion, which, again, because of their massive social media followings, was a huge win for us. We gave them a lot of creative license in designing the line's marketing campaigns, and they would pick everything from the shoot location to the photographer, stylist, and props used. They conceptualized the campaigns start to finish and were even involved in the final selection of which photos to publish. We wanted them to have a real sense of ownership over what we were crafting together, and their excitement about these creative endeavors was noticeable.

The result was a partnership that was intentional, enthusiastic, and authentic. This trifecta was a strong hint to the direction we needed to move in—toward true co-creation. This model was something that we would replicate with other celebrity and creator collaborations going forward, allowing us to effectively test our thesis that authentic co-creation requires genuine partnership connection and shared values.

The Jenner effect was not the only time Pacsun saw success with a celebrity collaboration prior to the bankruptcy filing. I'd like to highlight a few other examples of note. Each one was another data point that we could refer to as something done right to help us map out our next steps.

Jerry Lorenzo and F.O.G.

Jerry Lorenzo's collection for Pacsun is another example of mutual benefit through creative collaboration. Prior to our collaboration, the designer had already achieved success with his Fear of God brand. Now, he was looking to Pacsun as the perfect partner to connect with younger audiences. In collaboration with Pacsun, he created his F.O.G. line, a more accessible option designed with youthful consumers in mind.

The response was significant, with the first delivery of F.O.G. product quickly selling out. In February 2016, Pacsun posted on Instagram announcing that a second delivery, featuring a coveted Guns N' Roses tee, was set to drop in April. The comments section hints at the excitement. User @dannnyflores wrote, "When it comes we're going!! 😩😍 @na.nnii." Other users similarly alerted their friends to the drop, with @simonepark writing, "@stephen_b gotta go early again," @_juniormarquez commenting, "@malikgoode_ let's get it," and @deeefernandez writing, "@araya10 as soon as it comes out I'm getting this 😻."[29]

As with the Jenners' line, this moment also saw our consumers getting involved with personal reviews and product hauls. @mikeyartc commented on the aforementioned Instagram post: "Curious on the

29 Pacsun (@pacsun), "@JerryLorenzo in @FOG Fear of God #collectionone," Instagram post, February 24, 2016, https://www.instagram.com/p/BCJfzFwRpsB/.

FOG line? I did a couple reviews and fitting. My YouTube in my profile/ bio." Again, it was an early nod to how our community was getting involved, with excitement about a genuine cultural moment inspiring customers to go beyond being consumers to being creators themselves.

Lorenzo's collaboration with Pacsun also caught the eye of mainstream media. A 2015 *Complex* magazine article sets the stage for the moment nicely:[30]

> About a week ago, Fear Of God founder and designer Jerry Lorenzo lit up Instagram with a caption nearly 42 weeks in the making. Speaking to an anonymous fan, Lorenzo explained that while he wanted to create clothing that his younger fans could afford, the costs of producing Fear of God apparel made that plan difficult to bring to reality.
>
> "On Instagram you have these followers that just don't understand that process and it hurts when they're like, 'Oh, you're saying that you're doing this for the kids, but your prices are crazy' and that stuff bothers me," Lorenzo recently told us over the phone.
>
> So, when Lorenzo was approached by PacSun—a retailer that Lorenzo believes connects directly to his younger fans—to create a more accessible interpretation of Fear of God, Lorenzo jumped at the chance. With help from PacSun, F.O.G., which hits PacSun retailers exclusively on Dec. 11, was born.

F.O.G. proved a success, and Pacsun's collaboration with Lorenzo would continue for years. The initial Collection One line featured a mix of

30 Gregory Babcock, "Exclusive: Jerry Lorenzo Explains the Story Behind F.O.G., His New PacSun Collaboration," *Complex*, November 16, 2015, https://www.complex.com/style/a/gregory-babcock/jerry-lorenzo-fog-pacsun-interview-exclusive.

street-savvy styles—bombers, hoodies, and thermal shirts, a clear nod to what young people were seeking at a time when streetwear was gaining ground in the mainstream. And the style suited Pacsun's young shoppers. Ranging from $40 to $100, while above the price point of fast fashion products, the line was far more accessible than Fear of God, Lorenzo's main line, and created access for a new legion of fans.

Lorenzo acknowledged this himself in the interview with *Complex*, emphasizing his aim to create for a younger demographic. When he speaks about one key piece in the line, a red hoodie that takes inspiration from the eighties teen film *The Karate Kid*, he explains that although he wouldn't include sweatpants or a sweatshirt in Fear of God, because it wouldn't fit the brand's narrative, the red hoodie works for F.O.G. because it's "very youthful," a mentality that he suggests applies to all of the garments in the collection.

The designer then goes on to articulate his intentional approach to creating for a younger audience as an opportunity to experiment with new silhouettes and designers—not because they're cheaper or easier to mass produce but because they naturally sync to a younger audience's needs: "This is something that I created for where I believe this demographic is. It's not the luxury 'come down,' it's not that thought process," he says. "I haven't always had the resources to do that, but now I do. I'm not going to give you Fear of God at a low price. I'm going to give you something that I curated and designed for the kids." He added: "With PacSun it was great because it had a level of freedom that I don't really have with Fear of God, my main line. They have factories and relationships and they know how to make product at a low price without sacrificing the important things."

Lorenzo's recognition of Pacsun as an ideal conduit to younger audiences validated our emerging position as a cultural bridge—connecting established creators with the next generation of consumers who shared their values and aesthetic sensibilities. We were becoming known not just as a retailer but as a collaborative partner that could amplify authentic voices while maintaining creative integrity.

This partnership exemplified the strategic alignment we sought in all our collaborations—mutual value creation rather than transactional licensing. Lorenzo gained creative freedom, manufacturing expertise, and direct access to a demographically aligned audience, while Pacsun secured cultural credibility and authentic streetwear aesthetics that resonated with our community. The success demonstrated that when partnerships are built on shared purpose rather than opportunistic reach, both sides experience sustained growth and enhanced brand equity.

#BEEN #TRILL, Virgil Abloh, Matthew Williams, and Heron Preston

Recognizing the rising demand for streetwear among Pacsun's young audience, we pursued other collaborations in the vein of F.O.G. One noteworthy endeavor that epitomizes the way youth culture was impacting fashion is seen in our work with #BEEN #TRILL, a brand Pacsun partnered with in 2015. The streetwear brand described itself as "an art collective and DJ crew whose image and sound is defined by the frenzy of new youth culture found on the pages of the deep web and on the blocks of big cities."[31] Its members included Matthew Williams, Heron Preston, and Virgil Abloh. Known for its ear-to-the-street approach, #BEEN #TRILL gained a huge following that concentrated around a mix of art, culture, and music, built using Tumblr, music videos, mixtapes, and merch.

31 Jian DeLeon, "What Exactly Is #BEEN #TRILL and How Do I Explain It to My Parents?," *GQ*, January 2, 2014, https://www.gq.com/story/what-is-been-trill.

In a January 2014 article entitled "What Exactly Is #BEEN #TRILL and How Do I Explain It to My Parents?" *GQ* describes #BEEN #TRILL's special collection for Pacsun as "the brand's biggest mainstream moment … effectively making their logo-heavy gear readily available, and affordable."[32] While #BEEN #TRILL T-shirts were in the $100 range, the merch the collective created for Pacsun peaked at $85 for a hoodie. Pacsun's ability to make a pricier product more accessible, in line with the financial capabilities of a younger audience, was a clear draw for the #BEEN #TRILL team.

Again, this was a case of mutual strategic value. #BEEN #TRILL leveraged Pacsun's infrastructure, manufacturing relationships, and retail footprint to reach a broader audience without compromising its artistic vision, while Pacsun gained access to the collective's cutting-edge aesthetic and deep cultural connections within the art and music communities.

As Pacsun looked to the future, it sought to further the success of the #BEEN #TRILL collaboration, establishing independent partnerships with both Virgil Abloh and Heron Preston. Abloh collaborated with hip-hop artist Kid Cudi on the Mr. Rager tour collection for Pacsun. The limited edition four-piece capsule was released on the heels of Kid Cudi's 2017 Passion Pain & Demon Slayin' North American Tour.

A Reddit thread about the Mr. Rager tour collection with Pacsun gives some insights into consumers' reception of the line. User u/swag115 commented, "Currently have a white one, I'm going to try and buy a black one." User u/ThexFarrow asked, "So it will be at the store Thursday?" Meanwhile, u/asia272001 asked, "Are they releasing any female merch or just male?" to which u/Soccerpl replied, "They're

---

32 Ibid.

unisex" and the original poster, u/blondfold added, "it's under their men's section, technically. but yeah."[33]

These last comments hint at broader shifts ahead—a move toward more unisex fashions. Although not yet fully realized, Pacsun was already slowly developing this vision. More generally, these comments also hint at the halo effect that social discussions can have. An online comment section about when a product is going to hit stores suggests people are planning to get that product in person. This was something we would see years later, when the Astrid wash of Pacsun's Casey Low Rise Baggy Jean would go viral on Black Friday weekend, and Pacsun's brick-and-mortar stores saw people coming in to request "the TikTok Jean." Looking back, the patterns are clear. However, at the time, we were just starting to recognize them for what they were: early indicators of the careful listening and community-led approach that would eventually define our brand transformation.

As with the Jenners, it was extremely rewarding to see the way the #BEEN #TRILL creative team members' individual careers took off. Matthew Williams would go on to serve as the creative director of Givenchy for three years before leaving to start his eponymous fashion label. Heron Preston would continue to work with Pacsun—in November 2018, the Basketball Skateboards line, co-founded by Heron Preston and Jacuzzi, would drop in-store and online and lead to Pacsun's first international pop-up experience, a case study I'll write about in chapter 6. Preston went on to work a number of high-profile gigs for companies such as Nike and Calvin Klein, and in 2025, he announced that he had reacquired full and exclusive rights to his brand and was focusing on his own label. Finally, Virgil Abloh was

33 u/blondfold, "Mr. Rager x Virgil Abloh collab items coming to Pacsun. Online tomorrow, in-store Saturday," Reddit post in r/KidCudi, June 27, 2018, https://www.reddit.com/r/KidCudi/comments/8udhy4/mr_rager_x_virgil_abloh_collab_items_coming_to/.

appointed artistic director of Louis Vuitton's menswear collection in 2018. Sadly, he passed away only a few years after stepping into the role. We at Pacsun remain grateful for the pivotal role he played in inspiring our community and me personally with his boundless talent. We continue to support Virgil's partnership with the Fashion Scholarship Fund, providing scholarships to rising talent.

SEEDS OF CO-CREATION: WHAT WAS WORKING, AND WHAT WAS STILL MISSING

Looking back, it's evident that collaborations such as those with the Jenners, #BEEN #TRILL, Jerry Lorenzo, and Virgil Abloh were early seeds of Pacsun's future co-creation strategy. However, at the time, these collaborations were not yet part of a more cohesive, intentional move toward proactive co-creation. I would characterize them more as moments of reactive opportunity recognition than proactive cultural strategy. We were responding to individual partnerships as they emerged rather than building a comprehensive framework for authentic co-creation. Still, these were valuable learning experiences for the Pacsun team. Looking at these examples, a few commonalities can be seen in where we got it right.

Establishing Authentic Partnerships

Each of the collaborations described in this chapter speaks to a spirit of genuine creative input, giving Pacsun's collaboration partners creative license and ownership of the process. The Jenners exemplified this in their hands-on approach. Although they did not have fashion or design backgrounds, they were a big part of the process, participating in everything from fabric selection to fit feedback. That level of ownership made them eager to promote the outcome online, giving Pacsun authentic engagement and a major boost on social channels.

LESSON LEARNED: A true partnership is not in name only. Authentic collaboration requires holistic integration of partner perspectives throughout the entire creative process, not superficial brand association or licensing agreements. When creators have genuine ownership and decision-making authority, the resulting products naturally resonate with their communities, creating sustained engagement that goes further than temporary promotional moments.

Prioritizing Mutual Benefit

Partnerships such as those with Jerry Lorenzo exemplify the win-win that occurs when a collaboration is designed with mutual benefit in mind rather than as a transactional exchange. It wasn't just that these people were putting their names on Pacsun clothes; they were invited into the brand to exercise their creative freedom. In Lorenzo's case, he was able to reach a new audience through Pacsun's infrastructure, which made it possible to produce F.O.G. at a more accessible price point than Fear of God. Meanwhile, Pacsun benefited from Lorenzo's design expertise and established reputation in streetwear.

LESSON LEARNED: Strategic partnerships succeed when both parties experience genuine value creation rather than extractive arrangements that benefit only one side. Sustainable collaborations require deliberate planning to ensure each partner's core objectives are met through the relationship—whether that's audience expansion, creative freedom, manufacturing capabilities, or cultural credibility. This creates the foundation for long-term partnerships that evolve with both brands rather than transactional agreements that expire when immediate goals are achieved.

Serving as an Incubator for Emerging Voices

If you're going to shape the cultural conversation, not just participate in it, you have to look to new voices—the up-and-comers who may have a foot in the door but are not yet household names. We understood that cultural relevance required identifying and nurturing talent before it achieved mainstream recognition and positioning ourselves as a platform where such emerging creators could develop their voices and reach their intended audiences. Our work with #BEEN #TRILL was a testament to the value that can come with championing a counterculture brand. This strategic approach to incubation demonstrated our commitment to being culture catalysts, not culture followers.

LESSON LEARNED: When you deliberately create space for authentic voices to flourish instead of capitalizing on established trends, you can get ahead of cultural conversations, shaping them instead of following them. This requires thoughtful identification of emerging talent and an understanding that cultural leadership comes from strategic risk-taking on unproven voices rather than safe partnerships with established names.

Leaning into the Power of Social Media

Diverse as the collaborations described in this chapter may have been—the audience for the Jenners was very different from the #BEEN #TRILL audience, for example—all these partnerships spoke to the power of socials. The cultural relevance of moments such as F.O.G. did not just create social hype, however—they generated in-person and digital interest, creating a halo effect that saw a community of people emerge from behind their screens and coalesce in real-world spaces to participate. Social media served as the primary amplification channel for all our partnerships, creating a network effect in which authentic collaborations generated organic community engagement that transcended digital spaces.

LESSON LEARNED: When partnerships are built on genuine creative alignment rather than promotional tactics, social media becomes a catalyst for real-world community formation. People move from online conversations to in-store experiences because they feel connected to something meaningful. This early understanding of social media as a community-building tool, not just a marketing channel, laid the foundation for our eventual evolution toward comprehensive co-creation, where every stakeholder, from established creators to emerging community voices to customers themselves, becomes an active participant in shaping our cultural narrative.

THE MISSING PIECE: A CLEAR VISION, ROOTED IN A UNIFORM PURPOSE

The success stories described in this chapter got our consumer base excited, interested, and participating in dialogue with us, both online and offline, from interacting on social media to attending in-store events. However, these success stories alone were not enough to save the company from bankruptcy or rescue it after it emerged from bankruptcy.

So, what was still missing? The overarching gap was a clear brand strategy, informed by a cohesive purpose. A singular moment of success does not constitute a strategy, and a casual mission statement does not make a purpose. Pacsun still lacked its own brand identity. We hadn't yet articulated our co-creation strategy or defined our mission to inspire the next generation of youth by building community at the intersection of fashion, music, art, and sport. And while we were starting to dabble in these four pillars, they weren't yet connected in a cohesive way.

The lack of clear purpose was reflected in how we approached our collaborations. While they were successful in generating moments of genuine excitement in youth culture, they operated as individual successes rather than building blocks of a larger story. Without an overarching narrative to guide us, we found ourselves making partnership decisions based on opportunity rather than strategic alignment.

Today, we evaluate potential partnerships differently, asking: Do they share our values? Is there genuine, authentic connection with the brand? Why do potential partners want to reach our audiences? This strategic approach to partnership evaluation ensures that every collaboration strengthens our overarching narrative rather than creating isolated moments of success that don't build toward something larger.

Pacsun's lack of a clear, purpose-driven vision also continued to be seen in some of the other fissures I've discussed in previous chapters. There was the lack of clarity in terms of product: While Pacsun had been bringing in new brands that were deemed cool by younger audiences, such as Kendall & Kylie or Brandy Melville, it retained older brands that these consumers didn't have any affinity for. This was evidenced in the lack of cross-shopping we saw between trending and heritage brands, which I discussed in chapter 2. There was also a continued gap between the target audience for our men's and women's, with women's lines targeting twelve- to fifteen-year-olds and men's targeting eighteen- to twenty-four-year-olds. The effect was apparent when you walked into stores, where the merchandise sometimes gave the impression that our stores were places where big brothers and little sisters might shop together.

That external schism was mirrored from the inside out, as men's and women's were still largely siloed at this time. Within the company, there remained a spirit of competitiveness rather than collaboration. Teams were operating with different objectives and metrics, creating internal rivalry rather than aligned cooperation toward shared goals. This organizational fragmentation prevented us from leveraging the full potential of our successful partnerships, as each department optimized for individual performance rather than collective brand building.

The culture of Pacsun was fractured, and the path to coming together and reinventing itself couldn't begin until after the bankruptcy filing in 2016. To really transform the brand, we needed a new vision, and it had to be purpose-led. Following the bankruptcy filing and subsequent leadership changes, the opportunity was there to really let go of the past and focus on the future. The question then became: How would Pacsun define its purpose? The answer was surprisingly simple: Listen to the consumer.

CHAPTER 5

LISTENING LOUDER THAN EVER

BY 2017, PACSUN was well positioned to redefine the brand in a meaningful, modern way. The company had emerged from bankruptcy successfully, and a new era of leadership had been ushered in. The previous years had seen a number of noteworthy moments of cultural relevance, from successful brand partnerships, such as with Jerry Lorenzo, to popular celebrity collaborations, such as the Kendall & Kylie lines. The issue now became how to transform those singular moments of success into a cohesive strategy, informed by a clear vision.

So, how do you define your purpose? You need to look to someone who's far more powerful than any one C-suite executive will ever be: the consumer. Not until we started really listening to the consumer and engaging with the community around us, both our immediate LA community and the broader Pacsun community, were we able to evolve into the aligned, purpose-driven brand we are today.

It's not that we weren't listening to consumers before this point. We had recognized the importance of the consumer's opinion as far back as Project Mavericks, which had concluded that "The customer will be central to everything we do. Youth culture is created by teens, not adults, and we need to live and breathe their culture." And that recognition *had* carried over into action, evidenced by initiatives such as the Style Leader program—where we would handpick actual consumers from our stores (or, on some occasions, our competitors' stores) and ask them for real-world feedback about the brand.

The problem was that while we had feedback coming in, that feedback wasn't being elevated in a way that could actually shape the brand. For example, the Style Leader program feedback was incredibly siloed, staying primarily in the product departments. It was initially used by the design department to incubate new ideas and then extended to buying, with the buying teams having the style leaders come in and tell the teams about new products and brands.

Beyond design and buying, the style leaders weren't really leveraged in other departments, such as marketing. They certainly weren't viewed as a potential brand-building tool. It was more of a transactional approach; we were primarily interested in the information they could provide about the product, not the brand. Another problem was that the style leaders were an exclusive group, framed as the tastemakers of their generation. They only represented a small subset of our target audience, which resulted in a restricted point of view about what that audience might want. They did not represent the community as a whole.

These limitations were mirrored in our celebrity collaborations of the time. The people we partnered with were seen as emerging voices—tastemakers of the future—and invited to share their creative visions with our consumers. However, these collaborations still relied on a style leader of sorts, in this case a celebrity, and they were still dictating what was cool from the top down.

In short, we hadn't yet invited the consumers into the brand, which made it impossible to build a genuine community with them. We were still trying to tell our community what they should want rather than truly listening to what they actually *did* want.

From 2017 onward, this would change, and Pacsun would learn to enable co-creation not as an ancillary tool but as a core muscle that could be used to build the brand from the outside in. This shift would require not only building a modern feedback infrastructure but also mastering the discipline of authentic listening—because *really* listening means taking in the good and the bad, free of bias, and then acting on it while empowering others to act as well.

LEARNING TO LISTEN

Although the celebrity collaborations I discussed in the previous chapter weren't examples of true co-creation, they did teach us a lot—one thing being the power of social listening. The online conversations generated by these moments of celebrity-driven cultural reverence were buzzier and bigger than we'd anticipated, and the way they spilled over into the real world was incredibly exciting. As Pacsun's own social media presence grew, in part thanks to these collaborations, we were also getting more and more feedback. Now, we had the task of figuring out how to leverage it in a way that was actually meaningful. It would be a steep learning curve.

Building an Inclusive Feedback Structure

Initially—much like the Style Leader program—digital data was used primarily for pushing product. As far back as 2010, Pacsun had been exploring AI for predictive shopping. The problem was that the tech at that time was pretty rudimentary. For example, if a website visitor bought a green hoodie, the predictive tool would suggest five more green hoodies. Of course, the odds are that a person only needs one green hoodie. Today, you can see how these tools have evolved. If a person buys a green hoodie, a predictive shopping tool might instead suggest complementary items to complete the look, rather than five more green hoodies.

As these tools evolved, we evolved with them and eventually came to realize that instead of using data to predict what customers would want to buy, we were better off understanding how they actually wanted to express themselves. While some brands tried to dictate how people should dress, Pacsun saw its role as bringing unique pieces to market while welcoming customers to style them in their own unique ways.

This understanding that our consumers valued individual expression more than prescribed fashion was gleaned from intently listening to the consumer. Our multifaceted approach for soliciting their feedback included:

- **Using social listening:** Social media transformed our feedback loop from one-directional store reports to real-time, two-way conversations with engaged consumers across Facebook, Instagram, TikTok, Discord, and Reddit. Instead of waiting for store reports or consumer feedback surveys, we could access immediate reactions 24/7—customers would tell us exactly what they wanted, whether it was a product in a different color, larger sizes, or more of a specific item. This constant stream of authentic feedback became our most valuable research tool, allowing us to test concepts instantly and gather insights from the people who cared most about our brand.

- **Empowering our store associates:** We systematized store associate feedback through monthly visits, surveys, and weekly recap reports that captured the qualitative insights missing from sales data alone. While Monday sales reports showed what was selling, store teams provided crucial context, such as "A lot of girls have been asking for cropped versions of this sweatshirt" or "Customers like this fleece, but they want it oversized." This organized listening system ensured that frontline insights from customer conversations reached our design and merchandising teams in real time.
- **Giving our style leaders greater agency:** Our Style Leader program evolved beyond holding external feedback sessions to actively recruiting these authentic voices as full-time employees across the organization. One style leader I discovered at a competitor's store became our social media manager for nearly five years, resulting in genuine peer-to-peer communication rather than traditional brand-to-consumer messaging; she spoke the language because she lived the culture. Having actual customers run our marketing created authenticity that couldn't be manufactured.
- **Expanding beyond style leaders:** We broadened our listening network by regularly bringing in students from local high schools and colleges to provide ongoing feedback on products and concepts. This expanded approach helped us identify

individuals who consistently delivered spot-on insights, creating a pipeline of authentic voices who understood our community's evolving needs.

This more structured, inclusive approach to listening allowed us to gather insights from the broader Pacsun community—and to really understand what that community was looking for. With time, this would extend beyond our product and translate into other parts of the brand, helping to shape it as a whole—an evolution I'll discuss in the pages to come.

LESSON LEARNED: True community engagement requires systematic collection of diverse perspectives through multiple channels rather than relying on single feedback sources. When you create structured pathways for authentic voices—from social media conversations to store associate insights to direct customer panels—you build a comprehensive understanding of your community's evolving needs and can respond proactively instead of having to make reactive adjustments.

From Listening to Taking Action

It's important to distinguish between listening for the sake of listening and listening to actually do something with the information you get. True listening is a dedicated practice, not a onetime occasion, and it requires a dialogue—a response of some sort—for your audience to understand that their words are being heard. This would be the next pivotal step in Pacsun's evolution. Instead of cherry-picking from the feedback we got, focusing on the good or what was easy to fix, we took a more holistic approach. We had to take into account the good and the bad—and then we had to take action accordingly. That required really trusting the feedback that was being provided and empowering the people who were providing that feedback.

When I eventually stepped into the CEO role in 2023, this was something I made a priority from day one. Transitioning from having a strong personal point of view to truly empowering our community to guide our decisions required an intentional relinquishing of control. As someone whose background was rooted in product and creative direction, I had to learn to trust our teams and the feedback systems we'd built, even when they contradicted conventional retail wisdom.

More broadly speaking, learning to trust consumer insights over historical performance metrics was an organizational adjustment that required multiple iterations before it could be fully embraced. For example, we might have twenty girls tell us they didn't like a certain style of denim, but, historically, if that denim style had sold well, we would still decide to purchase and stock more of it based on the previous year's data.

LESSON LEARNED: True success happens when you trust the feedback and act on it, rather than simply acknowledging it while carrying on business as usual. This commitment to action requires both external and internal consistency—responding to every comment, positive and negative. Further, the way you present questions and gather insights must be intentional and unbiased, ensuring genuine dialogue rather than leading conversations toward predetermined outcomes. Ultimately, success depends on creating reliable systems where community feedback is allowed to directly influence decision-making.

Not Just Listening to Others—Empowering Them

When action is taken, it needs to be done efficiently and communicated clearly. Today, if our consumers tell us, "I love the wash of this jean, but I want them in a straight leg, not a bootcut," we will make that change quickly. That agility is possible because the external evolution of trust has been mirrored by an internal one, in which teams are empowered to act independently. Trust is one of our core values, and we trust our teams to make the right decisions in their departments. If a denim design is going to go from bootcut to straight leg, we trust the team to make the decision and implement the change.

This move toward greater empowerment mirrors our attitude toward co-creation, which has evolved as our approach to listening has evolved. Today, this goes far beyond product decisions. For example, social listening has made it possible to identify social media creators who are already highly engaged with the brand and mention it regularly. This opens a new window of opportunity, as these creators have the potential to be completely natural, authentic collaboration partners. Who better to partner with Pacsun than someone who is already authentically championing the brand? By empowering these voices, we empower ourselves.

This realization led to a fundamental shift in how we would curate our partnerships in the future, allowing us to establish creative relationships based on genuine connection to the brand rather than transactional reach. This approach defines our co-creation relationships to this day, shaping not only our celebrity engagements but also our broader community relationships. In the next chapter, I'll discuss how this inclusive approach to co-creation is being furthered with our community hub, which we launched in the fall of 2025.

LESSON LEARNED: Empowerment needs to be practiced both internally and externally, allowing teams to make rapid decisions in response to community feedback while simultaneously giving authentic brand advocates the creative freedom and platform to shape cultural conversations organically. Authentic co-creation emerges when brands empower voices that already demonstrate genuine connection rather than pursuing partnerships based solely on reach or influence metrics.

THROUGH LISTENING, BUILDING A COMMUNITY, AND FINDING A PURPOSE

As Pacsun started to really engage with its consumers, those interactions would shape much more than our product—they would come to shape our brand. Young consumers don't want transactional relationships with brands; they want authenticity, collaboration, and representation. They want a sense of community, the feeling that they are participating in something that aligns with their values. They want to be part of something bigger than themselves, whether it's participating in a cultural moment on social media or supporting a cause intended to make the world a better place.

Recognizing this, we knew that the conversations we were having with our consumers could no longer be limited to apparel. If we were going to really align with these younger generations, we had to get to know them more deeply than just asking, "Hey, what kind of jeans do you like?" Our community inspired us to start articulating what we cared about, well beyond fashion.

When we saw something that went against our values—say, the rise in hate crimes against the Asian American and Pacific Islander (AAPI) community—we spoke up. And, in line with what we had learned about really listening, we didn't just speak up; we took action. One initiative at a time, we developed into the purpose-led brand we are today. Here is a look at some of the moments when Pacsun led with purpose:

- **The UPRISERS #HATEISAVIRUS campaign and collaborative T-shirt:** This initiative was developed in response to a rise in violence against the AAPI community happening around the time of the COVID-19 pandemic, in 2020 and 2021. The campaign and T-shirt line, created in collaboration with the brand UPRISERS, launched in 2020, with all proceeds going to the Hate Is A Virus nonprofit in support of the AAPI community.
- **The Oto-Abasi Attah mural project:** This initiative was launched in 2020 after the George Floyd tragedy. We created a product collection with Inglewood-based artist Oto-Abasi Attah, who also created a mural for our Downtown LA store. The goal was to uplift and inspire the community to collectively work toward harmony and collaboration so that everyone could grow and heal.
- **Circulate Market:** The first iteration of the concept was a marketplace for black-owned brands, with proceeds going to different organizations handpicked by each brand partner. There have been other Circulate Markets since this first one, with a different theme for each (arts, education, etc.). The brains behind the concept is Corey Populus, the founder and creative force behind Circulate, an LA-based streetwear brand that blends fashion with culture and community storytelling. Circulate Market is the concept shop the designer curated to showcase and promote his own and other black-owned brands.

In taking a clear stance on such issues, Pacsun began to develop into the brand it is today: values-led and purpose-driven. With time and consistency, these initiatives created a foundation of trust among our community members that transcended traditional brand–consumer relationships. When your community sees you consistently taking meaningful action on issues that matter to them—not just during crisis moments but as an ongoing commitment to shared values—they begin to view your brand as a genuine partner in cultural change rather than a company trying to sell them products.

We are incredibly proud of the purpose-led company Pacsun has become and grateful to the community that helped us get here, and we continue to emulate this spirit today. For example, when the LA wildfires broke out in 2025, our teams immediately reached out via Instagram to community members who had lost their homes and everything in them to send overnight packages of clothing customized to their style and size. This authentic responsiveness builds the kind of loyalty that can't be manufactured through marketing campaigns.

Our commitment to our purpose further extends to every partnership we pursue. While our partnerships may once have been focused primarily on meeting demand for a certain type of product or extending our reach as a brand, they are now driven by a commitment to shared values. For example, our collaboration with Rare Impact Fund channels proceeds directly to Selena Gomez's mental health foundation—not because she's famous but because we share her values. This values-first approach to partnerships naturally evolved into our systematic co-creation model, in which authentic alignment has become the foundation for genuine creative collaboration.

STILL LISTENING TODAY, LOUDER THAN EVER

Pacsun's evolution from a brand dictated from the inside out to a community-based brand shaped from the outside in is a testament to the power of listening—*really* listening. We have come a long way since asking individual style leaders, "Which trends are you noticing?"

Today, the conversations we are having with our young co-creators go well beyond fashion.

This evolution was epitomized with the debut of Pacsun's first Youth Report, released in the fall of 2025. Created by GlobalData, an independent provider of data, analytics, and insights, the report, entitled *Pacsun: Deep Dive into the Youth*, offered unfiltered feedback from some six thousand Gen Z and Gen Alpha participants, covering everything from finances to mental health and career aspirations.

With this report, we really wanted to figure out what matters to the young people who form the basis of our community so that we can more effectively serve as an outlet for their voices. We aren't just listening to them; we want to help them be heard more widely so that we can support them in building the future they want—and from what we're seeing, they want a future that's just as purposeful as they are. For anyone who thinks young people are just concerned with scrolling social media without a care in the world, consider these insights:[34]

- **Concern for mental health outpaces physical health:** Among those surveyed, 42 percent claim that mental health is most important in their life right now, compared with 12 percent who state the same for physical health. This generation has grown up in a social media–orientated world, with many experiencing negative side effects due to overuse. Nearly one in five admits to being addicted to social media.
- **Individualism and a sense of self are especially important to Gen Z:** There is a general reluctance to being molded by external influences, particularly among Gen Z, as 32 percent

34 *Pacsun: Deep Dive into the Youth Report 2025* (GlobalData, 2025), independent research prepared for Pacsun.

of those surveyed claim that they themselves are the biggest influence on how they think, feel, or make decisions.

- **Feelings of anemoia persist:** Anemoia, a yearning for a past that you never actually experienced, is a common feeling among the youth surveyed. These feelings are in part driven by the fact that they have lived through challenging times in recent years, with both political and economic instability, as well as the recent COVID-19 pandemic.

As these younger generations forge their way forward, Pacsun wants to be in lockstep with them—listening to their concerns, amplifying their voices, and creating platforms where they can drive meaningful change rather than simply informing our product decisions. They helped us co-create a brand; now, how can we, together, co-create the future, not only of the Pacsun brand but beyond that? I admit, that's a huge question for any one person or brand to attempt to answer. And that's why we know we can't do it alone. It has to be a community effort.

Toward that end, we launched the Youth Report at our first Pacsun Purpose Partner Summit in the fall of 2025, with the aim of creating a physical space where digital conversations could translate into real-world collaboration and action. The event brought together our creator community with a selection of our purpose-driven partners, including Rich Orosco, chief brand officer at the Los Angeles Football Club (LAFC); Gavin Mathieu, founder and creative director at Supervsn Studios; and Heidi Zuckerman, CEO of the Orange County Museum of Art and author of *Why Art Matters: The Bearable Lightness of Being*.

We've found that music is incredibly important to Pacsun's community, so the event included a special music panel, featuring

Christy Castillo Butcher, SVP of programming at SoFi Stadium and Hollywood Park; Alex Joffe, who works on global partnerships at C3 Presents; Adam Roth, EVP of global partnerships and business development at The Recording Academy; and Phylicia Fant, global head of music industry and culture collaborations at Amazon Music. The panel was moderated by Tamala Lewis from AEG and it explored how brands and institutions can effectively connect with younger generations through co-creation, putting music at the forefront and showing up in meaningful ways by aligning with collaborations and the cultural spaces where young people already gather.

Also in attendance: Lyla Biggs. Her Instagram post about the Summit captures the spirit of the event beautifully: "AM I STILL DREAMING? I had the HONOR of getting the chance to speak at Pacun's first Purpose Summit a few weeks ago! Thank you SO much @pacsun and the INCREDIBLE team for believing in me & these cool kiddos- I am forever grateful to be a part of a generation shaping what's next 🫶."[35]

At the Pacsun Purpose Partner Summit, we also announced the establishment of the Pacsun Youth Advisory Council—another concrete step in amplifying our community's voice. The mission of the Youth Advisory Council is to empower Gen Z's and Gen Alpha's authentic youth voices inside Pacsun, driving innovation through co-creation and strengthening our joint purpose and community impact. This represents our most intentional approach to community co-creation yet, featuring twelve to fifteen members aged sixteen to twenty-two from Gen Z, plus two dedicated seats for twelve- to fifteen-year-olds representing Gen Alpha voices.

---

35 Lyla Biggs (@lylabiggs), "AM I STILL DREAMING? I had the HONOR of getting the chance to speak at Pacun's [sic] first Purpose Summit a few weeks ago!" series of ten Instagram photos, October 3, 2025, https://www.instagram.com/p/DPUydIRjTcV/.

Council members serve one-year terms, with opportunities for renewal and internship pathways, providing advisory input across five key tracks that align with our brand pillars: fashion, music, arts and design, sports, and community and purpose. We deliberately curate diversity across multiple dimensions—background, geography, and forms of creative expression—drawing from creators and cultural leaders across these pillars. Members include student leaders, store associates, and community youth partners, ensuring we capture perspectives from both our existing network and emerging voices who represent the future of youth culture.

The Youth Report and the Pacsun Purpose Partner Summit initiatives are just two examples of ways Pacsun is actively sustaining its dialogue with its community. The Summit was such a success, we plan to have one every year going forward to celebrate our brand partnerships and further unite our community. In the next chapter, I'll look at how this dialogue-driven approach to building community has extended to our partnerships with creators. I'll also reveal how our newly established digital community hub is democratizing creative processes even further, creating pathways for *any* community member to move from passive consumer to active creator—transforming the very definition of what it means to collaborate with a brand.

CHAPTER 6

WHEN CREATORS BECOME COLLABORATORS

AS PACSUN'S COMMUNITY has become more intentionally collaborative, the platforms we've become active on have proliferated. We're everywhere our consumers are: Instagram, TikTok, Substack, Discord, Pinterest, Reddit. That doesn't mean we're doing the same thing on every platform, as we're always adapting content and the conversation to the audience a specific medium attracts—what works on X won't work on Pinterest, for example. In some ways, the proliferation of platforms has further democratized the brand, allowing access to anyone and everyone, whatever their medium of choice may be.

That democratization is also evident in how we interact with creators on these platforms. It's no longer a matter of Pacsun, the authoritative brand, pushing content at its followers. Our community is invited to take part and create content alongside us. The Pacsun Collective is one example of this. Formally launched in 2024, the Pacsun Collective brings together our community of content creators, photographers, videographers, stylists, designers, musicians, and digital artists to join Pacsun's creative process and help shape future campaigns and merchandise. The movement was unveiled with the launch of our Spring/Summer 2024 Campaign, which was co-created with the brand's in-house creative team and a curated selection of community visionaries. These community members played a pivotal role in bringing the campaign to life.

Going forward, the Pacsun Collective offers an opportunity to truly co-create and community-source the future stages of the brand. We are excited to see what we can build with the diverse talents and voices that make up our incredible community—and we remain committed to listening as our primary tool for ensuring these collaborations stay true to our shared purpose of empowering individual expression while building community at the intersection of fashion, music, art, and sport.

This move toward genuine co-creation—a step away from hierarchical brand messaging and toward democratic dialogue—is also apparent in co-creator relationships beyond the Pacsun Collective. We are seeing everyday users become Pacsun ambassadors, championing the brand on social media in real, raw, and relatable ways. Think of Lyla Biggs, who helped spur Astrid's viral moment on that Black Friday weekend in 2023. The video that went viral was simple, shot in her bedroom at home—that was what resonated with our community.

This reflects some broader trends across Gen Z and Gen Alpha social media users, who seem to be shying away from the highly curated, picture-perfect images that once populated Instagram. Younger audiences aren't looking only to professional models or celebrities for inspiration anymore; they want to get it from someone like them, from their community or close to it. As of mid-2025, the social media posts that were driving the most engagement for Pacsun weren't those featuring polished, poised models. They were the ones that we reposted from our store associates or brand ambassadors (everyday consumers), who had posted organic content on their platforms. This shift isn't exclusive to our brand—it's one that's being driven by consumers. However, while some brands may shy away from allowing their consumers to tell their brand story, Pacsun has leaned into this opportunity.

Our shift toward authentic, user-generated content represents a deliberate strategic pivot—we are intentionally prioritizing community voices over polished brand messaging because we've learned that genuine peer-to-peer recommendations drive deeper engagement than traditional advertising. Our data consistently shows that authentic content from real customers creates stronger community connections and more sustainable growth than highly produced campaigns, so we've built our content strategy around amplifying these organic brand advocates rather than creating artificial moments.

Demetra, a creator we worked with in July 2025, exemplifies this approach perfectly. Her authentic college student perspective resonated so powerfully with our community that we saw follower growth spike by 41 percent week over week, with nearly two million TikTok views and thirty-one million Instagram views from her content alone. This wasn't manufactured virality; it was genuine connection between a creator who authentically embodied our brand values and a community that recognized that authenticity. The immediate sales spike and sustained engagement proved that when we partner with creators who genuinely represent our community, we achieve both cultural relevance and measurable business impact.

As our relationships with creators have evolved, who we collaborate with has become more all-encompassing. We aren't partnering exclusively with celebrities, as we did in the early 2010s, when famous faces were *the* tastemakers of the time. Our research suggests that today's youth are more influenced by their close-knit community and friends than by celebrities. So, when we do partner with celebrities, it's done intentionally, not because they're famous but because they align with our brand and its purpose.

Whether we work with a celebrity, a brand partner, or a creator, the bottom line is the same: We want to co-create with individuals and organizations whose values align with our own. That purpose-driven approach has opened up new opportunities—for both Pacsun and Pacsun's collaborators—that go far beyond promotional exchanges to create genuine platforms for creative expression, community building, and social impact that benefit all parties involved.

A CREATIVE REVOLUTION: FROM TRANSACTIONAL TO TRANSFORMATIONAL

In chapter 4, I discussed some of our earlier celebrity and brand partnerships, from #BEEN #TRILL to the Jenner sisters. We learned a lot from these success stories: the importance of authentic partnerships, the power of mutually beneficial collaborations, the value of serving as an incubator for emerging voices, and, of course, the benefits of leaning into social media. Most significantly, these early success stories gave us an idea of what was possible when authentic collaboration moved beyond surface-level brand association to genuine creative partnerships driven by shared value creation.

As Pacsun developed into a purpose-led brand, we could imbue our partnerships with new meaning, creating thoughtful approaches to co-creation that could scale authentic community engagement while maintaining those same genuine connections that made our early partnerships successful. This allowed us to step fully into our modern mission: to inspire the next generation of youth, building community at the intersection of fashion, music, art, and sport. Here's a look at some of the moments when we achieved that aim.

A$AP Rocky Shuts Down the Streets of SoHo

A$AP Rocky collaborated with Pacsun as our guest artistic director for two years, starting in 2021. What made this moment stand out to me was Rocky's genuine nostalgia for the Pacsun brand. He could remember shopping at Pacsun when he was younger, and he articulated a desire to bring the brand to the next generation of youth, including his own children. This wasn't just a brand collaboration for him. It meant something.

Rocky's first collection for Pacsun featured a reworked Vans Old Skool sneaker, a nod to our surf-and-skate past but with a fresh, streetwear twist. The fact that this was covered by *Billboard*, typically a music trade magazine, speaks to how Pacsun was gaining relevance in the broader cultural conversation through such relationships. From the *Billboard* article: "The nostalgic but forward-thinking collection is the Harlem rapper's latest fashion drop since taking on the role as Pacsun's Guest Artistic Director. Featured in the collaboration are reworked versions of the classic Vans slip-on sneakers and Vans slip-on mules, which are available in black and white colorways and multi-color flame designs."[36]

---

36 Latifah Muhammad, "A$AP Rocky Drops Latest Collaboration with Pacsun," *Billboard*, January 18, 2022, https://www.billboard.com/shop/asap-rocky-pacsun-vans-collaboration-1235020150/.

Rocky's role also included brand campaigns and in-store activations. In August 2021, Pacsun hosted a VIP launch party at its SoHo flagship store in New York City to celebrate the newest drop of A$AP Worldwide's collaborations with Russell Athletic and Vans. Rocky performed live at the store, exclusively previewing songs from his forthcoming album. The space was packed, with crowds lining up outside to get in. For those who couldn't make it in person, we also held a live-stream shopping event, giving customers around the world a first look at the new collection.

This was a case study in what happens when a well-articulated brand purpose meets the perfect collaborator. We trusted Rocky's creative process and gave him the tools he needed—even agreeing to change the *s* in Pacsun to a dollar sign for the big launch. If you look at photos from the SoHo event, you'll see the store's Pac$un signage.

LESSON LEARNED: This collaboration demonstrated the power of systematic trust-building in creative partnerships—when you identify collaborators with genuine brand connection and shared values, empowering them with creative freedom and operational support creates authentic cultural moments that resonate far beyond traditional marketing reach. Rocky's willingness to invest his artistic reputation in our brand, combined with our commitment to supporting his vision even in unconventional ways, such as changing our signage, proved that purpose-driven partnerships can generate sustained cultural relevance while driving measurable business impact through community engagement rather than manufactured buzz.

Emma Chamberlain and Pacsun Enter the Metaverse

Creator Emma Chamberlain was another example of a Pacsun partner who demonstrated authentic brand connection rooted in genuine nostalgia and shared values rather than transactional opportunity. She was genuinely excited to work with us and discussed her nostalgic affinity for the brand in an interview with *Teen Vogue*, saying, "I grew up shopping at Pacsun from the time I hit middle school through high school, and it's such a part of my childhood. To this day, they have amazing pieces that I love and wear. For me, nostalgia is something that hits hard—anything that has memories like Pacsun does, hits hard."[37]

Emma's enthusiasm translated to a multifaceted collaboration. We featured "Emma's Picks" on our website, highlighting items that she had personally flagged as her favorites from our latest product mix. She was also active in suggesting ideas for design, including a monogram collection. And she even entered the metaverse with us, as her second Pacsun collection debuted with a virtual reality experience starring Emma's digital self in the metaverse. The launch was complemented by the release of *Pacsun the Game*, which allowed users to explore underwater worlds along with Emma's virtual self.

Today, Emma has stepped back from certain social media platforms to prioritize her advocacy work, leaving behind platforms she found toxic and embracing those she experiences in a more positive way. It's a refreshing reminder that her values align with those of our community, as her advocacy for mental health awareness and her conscious approach to social media usage reflect the prioritization of mental health seen in our 2025 Youth Report.

LESSON LEARNED: Emma's partnership demonstrated how authentic collaborations emerge when creators and brands share not just aesthetic alignment but fundamental values around community well-being. Her consciousness around platform choice and mental

---

37 Gianluca Russo, "Emma Chamberlain on Her Second Pacsun Collection & Joining the Metaverse," *Teen Vogue*, February 22, 2022, https://www.teenvogue.com/story/emma-chamberlain-pacsun-ss22-interview.

health informed our own strategic decisions, notably our investment in Pinterest as a more positive space for our community.

Anna Sitar Live Streams the Super Bowl

In 2022, Anna Sitar and Pacsun partnered for the TikTok creator's live stream of the Super Bowl. While Sitar never explicitly mentioned the brand, she did wear a Pacsun sweatshirt. The subtle nature of the collaboration earned accolades from advertising industry trade magazine *AdAge*. An article entitled "The Top 5 Brand TikToks You Need to Know About Right Now" opens with "Pacsun didn't have a Super Bowl ad this year, but it did show up for the game on TikTok," before going on to unveil the partnership with Sitar.[38]

The following year, we invited Sitar to take over Pacsun's TikTok account directly and host a live stream shopping experience for our newly launched brand shop. Afterward, she headed to the big game, where she gave her community inside access to the event, providing highlights throughout the day. Our collaboration with Anna proved so successful, we ended up working with her repeatedly, even doing a full swimwear line together, and she now sits on our Youth Advisory Council.

LESSON LEARNED: This partnership exemplified our strategic shift toward authentic integration rather than obvious promotional content—Anna's genuine enthusiasm for the brand came through in how naturally she incorporated Pacsun into her content, creating the kind of peer-to-peer endorsement that resonates with younger audiences (who can quickly detect forced collaborations). The

---

38 Erika Wheless, "The Top 5 Brand TikToks You Need to Know About Right Now," *AdAge*, February 24, 2022, https://adage.com/article/special-report-creativity-top-5/top-5-best-tiktok-videos-brands-ranked-february-23-2022/2401801/.

sustained success of our relationship, evolving from subtle brand integration to product lines, further demonstrated how such authentic partnerships create long-term value.

Storm Reid Featured In Vogue

In 2022, Pacsun collaborated with *Euphoria* star Storm Reid to drop a swimwear collection. This was yet another case of genuine enthusiasm for the brand shining through. Speaking with *E! News* about the drop of her swimwear line, Reid stated, "I've been shopping at Pacsun for such a long time. I'd get allowance money or my mom would give me some money to go to the mall with my friends and we'd all stop and go to Pacsun because they, of course, obviously carry so many different brands that feel young and fresh and free and there's things for everybody and I think that's really important."

Reid's swimwear line was such a hit, it was featured in *Vogue* magazine, where she emphasized how hands-on she was in the design process, making sure to create swimwear for every body type: "If I didn't like something or felt like it wouldn't fit a certain body type, we would add extra hardware or extra support, or take things away. ... I was super involved in the [design] process."[39] Her commitment to inclusive design—ensuring every piece would flatter and support different body types—reinforced our understanding that authentic co-creation requires partners who share our values of accessibility and representation.

LESSON LEARNED: Reid's hands-on approach to modifying designs for broader body inclusivity demonstrated that meaningful collaboration

39 Christian Allaire, "Storm Reid on Her New Swimwear Line and What She's Wearing This Summer," *Vogue*, July 1, 2021, https://www.vogue.com/article/storm-reid-pacsun-swimwear-line.

extends beyond creative input to encompass the fundamental values that guide product development. This partnership affirmed for us the importance of creating genuinely inclusive experiences rather than surface-level diversity initiatives.

Heron Preston Spearheads Pacsun's First International Pop-Up

Pacsun had already been working with Heron Preston since his #BEEN #TRILL days. The collaboration continued with the launch of the Basketball Skateboards line, co-founded by Preston and Jacuzzi, which dropped in-store and online in November 2018. This innovative partnership took Pacsun's past affinity for surf and skate and paired it with a more current interest in streetwear, as it took inspiration from nineties skate culture and basketball.

The Basketball Skateboards line led to Pacsun's first-ever international pop-up experience, through a partnership with luxury department store Selfridges London, its flagship store. A skate ramp was included in the store, and Preston himself skateboarded. The Selfridges moment would hint at future changes to come, as Pacsun would eventually evolve beyond the B- and C-malls it had inhabited in the past to the A-malls most of its stores call home today—a development I'll delve into deeper in the next chapter.

Shortly after, Preston's show at the 2019 Paris Fashion Week was covered in *The New York Times*, a nod to the way streetwear had entered high fashion.[40] The article, which also covered Virgil Abloh and Matthew Williams, was entitled "They Been Trill. Now the Rest of the World Is, Too," a nod to the way the #BEEN #TRILL

---

40 Matthew Schneier, "They Been Trill. Now the Rest of the World Is, Too," *The New York Times*, January 16, 2019, https://www.nytimes.com/2019/01/16/fashion/heron-preston-paris-mens-fall-2019.html.

collaboration had been helping to shape cultural conversations well before hitting the mainstream. It was a reminder that long-term partnership development creates compound cultural value that extends far beyond individual product launches.

LESSON LEARNED: Our sustained relationship with Heron from #BEEN #TRILL through Basketball Skateboards demonstrated how systematic collaboration with authentic voices can open doors to new markets, elevated retail partnerships, and mainstream cultural recognition. This evolution from underground streetwear to luxury department stores and fashion week coverage proved that when brands invest in a creator's growth over time, both parties benefit from shared cultural elevation and expanded reach.

EXAMINING THE REASONS BEHIND THE SUCCESS STORIES

From A$AP Rocky shutting down the streets of SoHo to Emma Chamberlain entering the metaverse, instances such as these show how a cultural moment can create a lasting memory for the consumer while also generating genuine affinity for the brand. As Pacsun has become recognized as a voice for youth culture, we have been actively approached by other institutions seeking to connect with our purpose-led community, from Formula 1 racing to The Metropolitan Museum of Art.

As we have come to articulate what our brand stands for, truly listening to our consumers to shape that vision, we have been able to lean into purpose-led leadership. This has fundamentally reshaped who we are as a brand, allowing us to:

- **Identify collaborators with an authentic love for Pacsun:** Any one of the case studies discussed in this chapter speaks to this. Emma Chamberlain may have summed up the power of such connection best: "For me, nostalgia is something that hits hard—anything that has memories like Pacsun does, hits hard."
- **Develop partnerships driven by creative freedom, where genuine input is prioritized:** While we still require aesthetic alignment in terms of product—we are a casual brand, not luxury—we don't limit our creative partners. If A$AP Rocky wants to change Pacsun to Pac$un for his event, we'll do it, because we trust his vision.
- **Partner exclusively with people, organizations, and brands that share our values:** From Emma Chamberlain's focus on mental health to Storm Reid's calls for inclusive swimwear, we work exclusively with collaborators whose missions align with our commitment to community empowerment, accessibility, and positive cultural impact. This values-first approach ensures that every partnership strengthens our overarching purpose rather than creating disconnected promotional moments.
- **Create moments of cultural relevance:** Strategic partnerships such as Heron Preston's Basketball Skateboards line, which led to our first international pop-up at Selfridges London, demonstrate how authentic collaborations can open doors to elevated cultural spaces and new market opportunities. Pacsun remains committed to delivering experiences that transcend traditional retail boundaries by creating moments of cultural relevance people want to talk about and take part in.

- **Include our community more broadly:** To more broadly include our community in such moments of cultural relevance, we have created multiple touchpoints for community engagement around major collaborations, from virtual experiences for those who can't attend in person to behind-the-scenes content on TikTok and in-depth interviews through our PAC TV series "Two Minutes With" (for example, "Two Minutes With Emma Chamberlain"). These rapid-fire interview formats give our community intimate access to the people they admire while reinforcing the authentic connections that make these partnerships meaningful.

If there is one big takeaway from what Pacsun has learned as our relationship with co-creation has evolved, I think it's to simply trust your customer—put them in the driver's seat. This has meant relinquishing traditional brand control and empowering our community to choose when and how they engage with us, rather than dictating those interactions through predetermined campaigns. We've discovered that when creators and customers self-select partnerships because they genuinely love the brand, the resulting content and engagement is exponentially more authentic and impactful than anything we could orchestrate.

That community-first approach also contributes to the democratization of the creator economy, which we are proud to support. When moments such as those with Lyla Biggs or Demetra happen, they aren't just a big deal for Pacsun. They're also a big deal for the creator, who can benefit financially. For Pacsun, that creator can be anyone who loves the brand. There's no formal approval process. If someone wants to share their love for Pacsun, we welcome them to do so.

LOOKING AHEAD: EXPANDING ACCESS WITH PACSUN'S OWN COMMUNITY HUB

I believe this shift toward community-driven collaboration—where influence comes from genuine connection rather than follower count and where creators build their own revenue streams through authentic brand advocacy—represents the future of sustainable brand building. With this shift in mind, Pacsun began exploring how to create infrastructure that could support and amplify community creativity on a much larger scale.

In the fall of 2025, we launched our own community hub, PS Hub, our most ambitious step toward true co-creation to date. Hosted directly on pacsun.com, the hub allows us to connect with our community on our own terms, no third-party platforms needed. On this interactive platform, our community can exchange creative ideas and opinions. For example, aspiring designers can upload their ideas for community feedback and get potential partnership opportunities with Pacsun, while creators can engage with our ecosystem, participate in community initiatives, and access behind-the-scenes content.

Eventually, the platform will integrate shoppable features and live social commerce capabilities, allowing Pacsun lovers to engage directly with live streams and post their own content rather than relying solely on external platforms such as TikTok. This approach gives our community greater access to Pacsun, allowing members to proactively shape their experience with the brand—and, in the process, shape the brand itself. You can see it for yourself:

For Pacsun, it's another building block in our mission to keep listening louder than ever. The data we get from the community hub's users can inform buying and design decisions, provide valuable community insights, and help us identify emerging trends and voices before they reach mainstream awareness. The end goal is to create our own community space while using other platforms as complementary channels, ensuring we maintain direct relationships with our most engaged community members regardless of how social media platforms evolve.

Pacsun's post-bankruptcy evolution has been significant and required great effort. So far, I've focused largely on how staying in constant conversation with our community helped redefine the brand from the outside in. At the same time, there were many strategic changes going on internally. In the next chapters, I'll continue the story of our transformation from a mall brand to a purpose-led retailer with serious digital muscle while also unpacking how an intentional shift in strategy on the inside mirrored what was happening on the outside. The community-driven brand transformation you've seen required equally dramatic changes to how we operated as a business—from our technology infrastructure to our organizational structure and fundamental approach to retail itself.

CHAPTER 7

BUILDING DIGITAL MUSCLE

PACSUN'S SHIFT TOWARD authentic three-way partnerships (Pacsun + brand partner + creator) has helped us shape the cultural conversation. We are no longer following the trends. We, in collaboration with our audiences, are helping to set them. This shift has also been pivotal in boosting sales. One noteworthy testament to this fact was seen in TikTok's Super Brand Day of 2024.

Super Brand Days are promotional events on TikTok Shop where a featured brand takes center stage, offering exclusive deals, interactive content, and live shopping experiences to drive sales and brand awareness. When Pacsun participated in the Super Brand Day in 2024, we became the number one seller on the platform during the four-day event, demonstrating how authentic creator relationships and strategic social commerce can drive significant business impact.

This success validated our investment in building genuine community connections rather than relying solely on traditional digital marketing. We had cultivated a network of creators and community members who were genuinely excited to champion our brand during this high-visibility moment because they identified with our purpose and aligned with our values. At the same time, we were powering the creator economy, giving champions of our brand the benefit of financial gain.

Just as it took years of careful planning to allow for the viral moment of the Astrid wash of the Casey Low Rise Baggy Jean in 2023, a carefully thought-out digital strategy paved the way for the 2024 Super Brand Day success. Here's a look at the key milestones that led up to this moment:

- **February 2020:** Pacsun launches on TikTok, featuring Mathieu Simoneau's post from Morocco.
- **August 2021:** Pacsun debuts its first live shopping event from its NYC SoHo flagship store, featuring an exclusive shoe drop from guest artistic director A$AP Rocky.
- **August 2022:** Pacsun hits two million followers on TikTok.
- **February 2023:** Pacsun makes its first sales on TikTok Shop through the platform's beta program. The live-stream shopping event was hosted during the Super Bowl, part of our collaboration with featured creator Anna Sitar.
- **November 2023:** The Lyla Biggs effect takes hold, a testament to how the creator economy can impact brands and creators alike.
- **February 2024:** Lyla content is now outperforming paid media campaigns.

- **December 2025:** By this point, Pacsun has sold one million pairs of the jean on TikTok Shop.

When compiled in a few bullet points, these milestones look straightforward enough. However, it took a thoughtful road map for Pacsun to become one of the "Top 10 Fashion Brands on TikTok," as named by *Women's Wear Daily* alongside Louis Vuitton, Dior, Gucci, and others.[41] While building its digital muscle, Pacsun was also evolving its brick-and-mortar stores, taking once transactional retail experiences and making them more interactional. Today, that dual evolution of our online and offline spaces has allowed Pacsun to combine online selling with the draw of authentic in-person experiences that bridge digital and physical touchpoints. This chapter looks at how we did it.

A DIGITAL EVOLUTION: FROM SOCIAL MEDIA TO SOCIAL SELLING

The transition from legacy brand to top fashion brand on TikTok required reimagining how we thought about digital platforms, customer engagement, and the relationship between online and offline experiences. While other brands saw social media as a marketing channel, we recognized its potential as a commerce platform and community hub. This shift in perspective allowed us to build our digital muscle and gain an early competitive edge in social commerce.

41 Alexandra Pastore and Kanika Talwar, "Top 10 Fashion Brands on TikTok," Yahoo! Lifestyle, September 13, 2024, https://www.yahoo.com/lifestyle/top-10-fashion-brands-tiktok-151500234.html.

Making an Early Bet on Social Selling

When Pacsun first got on TikTok in February 2020, the platform was largely seen in the US as little more than a dance app. Consider some of the media headlines about the platform at the time:

- **"5 of the Best TikTok Dance Challenges—and How the App Is Changing the Dance World"—*Dance magazine*:** "TikTok seems tailor-made for dancers. The app's short-form video format makes it easy to show off your best moves to a song that's gone viral. And an algorithm that favors unknown users means up-and-coming dancers have a better chance of reaching a large audience than they might on Instagram or YouTube. Dance challenges are especially popular on TikTok, with over one billion views for the hashtag #DanceChallenge alone."[42]
- **"Do I Need to Be on TikTok?—A Guide for Oblivious Thirty-Somethings"—*Axios*:** "Most of the videos lean on a bizarre brand of internet humor born from meme culture that's heavy on sarcasm and self-deprecation. You'll also see plenty of lip sync dubs (harkening back to the Musical.ly days), dance challenges, and common editing combos stolen and then tweaked without credit to the original creator (just like memes)."[43]
- **"How Charli D'Amelio Became the Face of TikTok"—*The New Yorker*:** "She is not an Instagram heiress, a world-class

42 Dance Spirit, "5 of the Best TikTok Dance Challenges—and How the App Is Changing the Dance World," *Dance Magazine*, September 19, 2019, https://dancemagazine.com/5-of-the-best-tiktok-dance-challenges-and-how-the-app-is-changing-the-dance-world.

43 Katie Levans, "Do I Need to Be on TikTok?—A Guide for Oblivious Thirty-Somethings," *Axios*, October 9, 2019, https://www.axios.com/local/charlotte/2019/10/10/do-i-need-to-be-on-tiktok-a-guide-for-oblivious-thirty-somethings-182376?.

> athlete, or a successful recording artist. Charli D'Amelio is a soft-spoken, Connecticut-bred high schooler who performs short dance routines, often in her bedroom. Since joining the app last spring, D'Amelio has amassed more than six billion likes and eighty-two million followers."[44]

Despite the popular framing of the app as primarily a space for sharing dance videos, we at Pacsun suspected it would eventually enter social selling. Douyin, TikTok's sibling app in China, had already spearheaded social selling, integrating e-commerce directly into the app's features in March 2018. This allowed Douyin creators with substantial followings to link products from retailers such as Alibaba's Taobao and Tmall platforms. The following year, Douyin introduced a shopping cart feature in time for 618, China's second-largest annual shopping festival.[45] It seemed clear that it was only a matter of time until TikTok followed suit.

Sensing what the dance app was aspiring to, Pacsun began preparing accordingly, even working with the TikTok team directly. In early 2020, Pacsun's chief technology information officer and I took a trip up to San José to sit down with the TikTok team. What we discovered was an opportunity to help build the platform's commerce infrastructure alongside their team. TikTok wasn't a retailer, so the team didn't know how to handle checkout processes or integrate backend systems. We worked behind the scenes to help develop what would eventually become TikTok Shop, positioning ourselves as a strategic partner rather than just another brand hoping to use the platform.

---

44 Cassidy George, "How Charli D'Amelio Became the Face of TikTok," *The New Yorker*, September 5, 2020, https://www.newyorker.com/culture/cultural-comment/how-charli-damelio-became-the-face-of-tiktok.

45 Rebecca Sentance, "What Brands Can Learn from China About Tapping Into TikTok's Selling Power," Econsultancy, August 23, 2021, https://econsultancy.com/what-brands-learn-china-douyin-future-tiktok-ecommerce/.

LESSON LEARNED: Sometimes, you have to take an early bet. The brands that succeed are the ones willing to invest time and resources in platforms before they become obvious opportunities. By the time everyone else recognizes the potential, you've already built the relationships and infrastructure that give you a competitive advantage.

Building an Agile Infrastructure

Pacsun's work with TikTok highlighted a distinct advantage: We already understood the fundamentals of digital commerce. While TikTok was learning about shopping carts, payment processing, and inventory management, we had been refining these capabilities for years. Still, it wasn't until 2020 that we really saw the online shopping boom. Like many retailers, the advent of the COVID-19 pandemic, which essentially shut down much of the world, led to tremendous growth in online sales. E-commerce sales increased 50.5 percent year over year from 2019 to 2020 and increased a further 14.2 percent year over year from 2020 to 2021.[46] Since 2020, e-commerce has continued to account for at least one-fifth of all US retail sales every year.[47]

Pacsun was well prepared to ride the momentum of this broader industry shift. When the pandemic first hit, we temporarily repurposed our brick-and-mortar stores and transformed them into shipping hubs, allowing us to send out inventory directly from these locations. This nimbleness was not only operational but also cultural. While other brands scrambled to figure out how to connect with customers

---

46 Jason Goldberg, "E-Commerce Sales Grew 50% to $870 Billion During the Pandemic," *Forbes*, February 18, 2022, https://www.forbes.com/sites/jasongoldberg/2022/02/18/e-commerce-sales-grew-50-to-870-billion-during-the-pandemic/.

47 Abbas Haleem, "US Ecommerce Sales in 2024 More than Double Those of 2019," *Digital Commerce 360*, March 3, 2025, https://www.digitalcommerce360.com/article/us-ecommerce-sales/.

stuck at home, we already had the infrastructure and mindset to meet our community where they were: online, creating content and seeking authentic connection during an isolating time.

Thanks to our agility, we were able to leverage live shopping and social commerce on TikTok and YouTube to engage with consumers, inspiring them to style new looks and participate in trends from home. Rather than seeing the pandemic as a pause, we saw it as an acceleration of the digital-first, community-driven approach we had already been building. This momentum paid off significantly: Today, over a third of our business is digital, which is higher than many of our competitors and a testament to our youthful consumer base that was already primed for this shift.

That agility also translated to what was happening internally at Pacsun. We recognized that to move at the speed our community demanded, we had to break down the internal silos that had historically defined our operations. This meant creating cross-functional think tanks, acknowledging that our best ideas could come from anywhere, at any level across the organization. The transformation was both structural and cultural, encompassing everything from an office redesign to a revisiting of Pacsun's core values—all of which I'll discuss further in the chapters ahead.

LESSON LEARNED: Agility requires an internal structure and culture that allows you to respond to opportunities in real time. If the unexpected happens (say, a global pandemic), having agile systems in place will enable your organization to pivot as needed. That agility needs to be infused into the organization at every level, reflected in empowered teams and intentional collaboration.

Testing New Approaches

Through the lens of Pacsun's social media collaborations, we were able to conceptualize a new approach to e-commerce, one rooted in a more direct dialogue with the consumer. Instead of simply presenting people with a website to browse and shop passively, we were inspired by the community we built through social media to create online shopping experiences that were immersive, engaging, and immediate. That generated excitement, and that excitement translated to sales, a fact that we witnessed well before the resounding success of the Super Brand Day in 2024.

For example, in 2021, we beta-tested our first live stream shopping event using a backend provider called Bambuser. This was part of the A$AP Rocky activation in SoHo, where Rocky debuted an exclusive shoe drop. Mathieu Simoneau from our first TikTok post in Morocco years earlier was there to host the live stream, which had thousands of views. The sales were impressive: I think we sold over two hundred pairs of shoes in the hour that Mathieu live streamed. That told us we were onto something.

Another, more recent, case study: Pacsun's Puerto Rico Swim Trip 2025. The campaign featured macro influencers creating brand stories with new products across TikTok, Instagram, and YouTube. The campaign resulted in $2.8 million earned media value—the estimated monetary value of the exposure a brand receives from unpaid mentions, shares, and engagement generated by influencers. We also saw 2.3 million total engagements, 43.5 million impressions, and a reach of 107 million, as well as more than 8,000 comments and some 2.5 million likes.

These results validated our early investment in social commerce infrastructure. At the time of this writing, in the last rolling twelve months, we've generated over $35 million in sales on TikTok Shop alone. While that's still less than 10 percent of our overall digital business, it's a significant starting point for expanding our presence. And what's most exciting is the customer data, which indicates that 95 percent of consumers we've attracted on TikTok over the past year are net new customers. This represents a powerful new customer acquisition channel, allowing us to expand our community while meeting customers where they are and establishing ourselves as first movers in social commerce.

Social commerce has proven to be the perfect meeting point for Pacsun's commitment to connection, community, and co-creation. By stepping into this space, we can meet consumers where they're actually spending their time, which is increasingly on social platforms, not traditional e-commerce sites. This trend is expected to continue. In 2022, the global social commerce market was valued at $728 billion, with a projected compound annual growth rate (CAGR) of 32 percent, expected to reach approximately $6.2 trillion by 2030. Meanwhile, the US social commerce market was valued at $89 billion with a projected CAGR of 30 percent, expected to reach approximately $660 billion by 2030.[48]

LESSON LEARNED: Behind every successful social commerce campaign is a foundation of authentic community relationships, strategic platform partnerships, and the infrastructure to capture and act on real-time data. You have to be willing to test, measure, fail fast, and iterate.

---

48 *Social Commerce Market Summary (2025–2033): Size, Share & Trends Analysis by Business Model (B2B, B2C, C2C), by Product Type (Personal & Beauty Care, Apparel, Accessories, Home Products), by Platform/Sales Channel, by Region, and Segment Forecasts* (Grand View Research, 2025), https://www.grandviewresearch.com/industry-analysis/social-commerce-market.

A BRICK-AND-MORTAR REVOLUTION: THE REVIVAL OF THE SHOPPING MALL

While Pacsun has been building its digital muscle, it's also evolved its brick-and-mortar presence. In 2025, Pacsun opened multiple new locations, strategically thought out and in line with consumer demands. With that said, we've carefully refined our approach to in-store shopping. Because, in truth, it's less about shopping and more about creating experiences.

Recognizing the Shopping Mall's Resurgence

When Pacsun filed for bankruptcy, its store fleet required restructuring. The bankruptcy allowed Pacsun to get out of expensive leases in underperforming locations—so-called B- and C-malls, which generally have a lower sales performance than A-malls. For example, while an A-mall may sell $1,000 per square foot, a B-mall may sell $500 per square foot. Other factors, such as tenant mix, location, and occupancy, also determine whether real estate professionals rank a mall as an A-, B-, or C-mall.

Today, Pacsun's stores are located primarily in A-malls—and that footprint is growing. However, this time, the growth is strategically thought out. Pacsun's founders and early management had driven growth largely through new store openings rather than same-store sales growth. Now, Pacsun is growing its brick-and-mortar presence in premium locations because it makes sense from a numbers standpoint—and from a cultural standpoint. Because the truth is that the shopping mall is making a comeback, something that few people anticipated.

There has been plenty of discussion about the death of the shopping mall, a cultural institution that seems to have peaked in the 1990s and early 2000s. The iconic Mall of America opened in

1992, featuring not only retail but also massive entertainment facilities. Meanwhile, the mall made appearances in pop culture movie moments from *Clueless* (1995) to *Mean Girls* (2004). Malls were even characterized as "the new Main Streets of America."[49]

As the market became saturated, the mall became a victim of its own success: By 2008, the US had more retail space per capita than almost any other country. The financial crisis and recession of 2007–2009, coupled with the rise of e-commerce, led to a decline in foot traffic in malls and the emergence of so-called dead malls.[50] Now, we are seeing those malls make a resurgence.

Retail research shows that occupancy rates are up, as is foot traffic. And it's largely Gen Z that is driving the resurgence.[51] That trend aligns with what we're seeing at Pacsun, where we've measured a 17 percent increase in foot traffic in the past year—significantly more than the average 3 to 5 percent other stores are seeing. In Pacsun's case, that increase in foot traffic is mirrored by a boost in conversions, an indicator that our young consumers aren't just setting foot in stores but spending money while they're there.

LESSON LEARNED: Don't write off the old. Instead, look for ways to reimagine and revitalize existing infrastructure to meet evolving consumer needs. Sometimes, the most innovative strategy is recognizing that what seemed outdated actually has untapped potential when approached with a fresh perspective.

---

49 Josh Sanburn, "Why the Death of Malls Is About More than Shopping," *Time*, July 20, 2017, https://time.com/4865957/death-and-life-shopping-mall/.

50 Matthew Wells, "The Economic History of the Shopping Mall—and Its Future (Yes, It Does Have One)," Federal Reserve Bank of Richmond: Econ Focus, Third Quarter 2022, https://www.richmondfed.org/publications/research/econ_focus/2022/q3_economic_history.

51 "Heading Back to the American Mall," *NPR*, December 18, 2023, https://www.npr.org/2023/12/18/1198909399/1a-draft-12-18-2023.

Understanding the New Role of the Shopping Mall

Curious about the uptick in in-store shopping, Pacsun surveyed members of Gen Z and Gen Alpha to find out more. What we discovered challenges traditional assumptions about retail motivation: Shopping isn't even the primary reason these young consumers visit malls. Rather, they are seeking community. For our consumers, the mall serves as a crucial third space—not home and not school but a co-owned cultural space where they can express themselves, connect with others, and participate in the trends they're creating online.

Pacsun decided to deliver on that demand by curating authentic opportunities for engagement in its brick-and-mortar spaces, from pop-ups to limited-time brand experiences that create a sense of FOMO and drive social sharing. Today, we're developing creator-led spaces where Gen Z influencers host product drops and in-person Q&As inside our stores. The same energy that made the Astrid jeans take off from Lyla's bedroom TikTok video is now happening in photo zones inside Pacsun locations.

In recognition of the rising significance of the mall, we even shot our fall 2025 Denim Days campaign in one. This was no chance decision. We chose it because that's where culture is happening, again. For Gen Z and Gen Alpha, the mall isn't a relic. It's a revival. As young people are coming back to the mall, they are bringing new energy with them. Our research is clear: Today's youth are drawn to the mall not just to shop but to connect, create, and express themselves in real life.

LESSON LEARNED: Listen to what your community members actually want, not what industry experts predict they should want. The narrative about the dead mall has been circulating in retail circles for years, and it hasn't been totally accurate. When we stopped assuming what consumers wanted and started asking them directly, we discovered they were seeking connection and cultural experiences—and that the mall was one conduit for delivering those.

Creating a Modern Mall Experience

Pacsun's research has shown us that while the younger generation may be digitally fluent, they want more than digital experiences. They care about live events, from music activations to fashion shows. They want the one-of-a-kind experience of seeing A$AP Rocky perform or meeting the Jenner sisters in person or skating with Heron Preston inside the Selfridges skate bowl in London. That drive for human connection, for a sense of community, hasn't changed.

That's why we've been doing things such as hosting "get ready with me" activations before New Year's Eve, offering hair and makeup for customers preparing for parties, and collaborating with Newport Run Club, inviting their members to meet in our stores pre-run. We've even started creating custom merch for each run club with their specific group name on it. We've also hosted creator marketplaces in our stores, where we don't sell clothes or make any money at all. Instead, we invite local artists and small brands to do pop-ups in our stores or parking lots, with 100 percent of proceeds going back to them and a charity of their choice.

These initiatives represent a fundamental shift in how we think about retail space. The mall, and more specifically Pacsun, isn't just a place to shop. It's a place to connect. When someone thinks back to their favorite mall experience, we want them to remember the time they got styled for their big night out, met there for a run, or discovered a local artist at our creator marketplace, not just the time they bought a pair of jeans. As the mall continues its cultural resurgence, that's the mindset we are leaning into.

LESSON LEARNED: Retail space is only as valuable as the experiences and memories it creates. By prioritizing genuine connection through initiatives such as creator marketplaces and styling sessions, you build the kind of brand loyalty that translates into long-term business success. Design spaces that serve consumers' real needs, turning stores into interactive community hubs instead of simple retail locations.

BLURRED LINES: BALANCING THE DIGITAL AND IN-PERSON WORLDS

While digital and brick-and-mortar remain distinct, we're increasingly seeing the lines between the two blur. An in-store activation will appear on social media, for example, while a social shopping event can get a boost from the real-time content of a relatable creator. This blurring of lines means we need to rethink how we approach our consumers and the experiences we create for them, both online and off.

The melding of digital and in-person spaces also has practical implications for Pacsun as a retailer. Remember, when Pacsun's "TikTok Jean" (Casey) went viral, there was a halo effect: We saw the social media interest spill over into stores, where the stock sold out. That experience taught us the power of real-time data. We reconsidered our approach to tracking supply and demand, as well as our entire infrastructure around efficiency. How could we remain nimble enough to avoid stockouts in a world where you can't know 100 percent what will go viral? This is where cutting-edge tech such as AI holds great promise.

In late 2023, I attended the D^3 Institute at Harvard, an invite-only HBS Alum gathering where global leaders discussed the future of AI, led by Professor Karim Lakhani. My biggest takeaway from that summit was that companies that don't embrace AI will become obsolete—the future Blockbuster or Kodak case studies business schools use when they talk about successful enterprises that fell behind. So, just as Pacsun once made an early bet on TikTok, it's now making an early bet on AI.

Following my time at the D^3 Institute, we rolled out an eighteen-month road map to incorporate AI into every part of our organization. One integration of note was the launch of our smart platforms—MondaySmart, PlanSmart, and InventorySmart—AI-powered tools for forecasting, allocation, and buying. These systems create a dynamic way to understand what's happening in our business at any given time. We can now make smarter inventory decisions, optimize allocation to specific stores, and access real-time results that previously would have taken weeks to compile.

The philosophy behind this mirrors our approach to co-creation: Human capital plus AI becomes our superpower, what Ethan Mollick calls "co-intelligence" in his book of the same name. Mollick was one of the guest speakers at the D^3 Institute summit at Harvard, and that is where I was given his book. In it, he frames AI as a "co-worker, co-teacher, and coach," not as a tool but as a collaborative partner. His concept of co-intelligence envisions a future in which AI is able to augment human ingenuity while humans remain in control. His principles for effective AI use are helping to guide our own approach at Pacsun: Invite AI to the table and experiment with its capabilities and limitations; keep humans in the loop and never lose oversight; treat AI as a human with a well-defined role; and, finally, assume AI is only going to get better.

Not every AI experiment we've run has worked; for example, we've turned off personalization and website optimization tools that didn't deliver results. But that's the point: We test, we measure, and we adapt quickly. This fail-fast approach will become even more important with new initiatives such as PS Hub, our own community hub. With our community consolidated in a space that we own, rather than a third-party social site, we can engage and interact more seamlessly, allowing for faster and more accurate data capture.

For example, if we tease something in PS Hub, the response can help us gauge potential virality and then make inventory decisions based on that information. The result will be much more algorithmic, with an AI backbone that identifies what has the potential to scale based on early community signals. This will allow us to pursue product appropriately and avoid both stockouts and overstock situations.

Our AI systems now help us understand not just what products are selling but where they are selling and why. When we see a spike in demand for a particular item on TikTok Shop, our algorithms can predict which physical stores are most likely to see similar demand based on demographic data, past purchasing patterns, and local social media engagement. This predictive capability has fundamentally changed how we stock and staff stores as well as how we plan their in-person events.

Perhaps most importantly, this integrated approach allows us to honor what our community is telling us through their behavior, not just their words. Far from removing the human from the equation, adoption of these tools allows us to fine-tune our human-first focus. What do consumers want? Where do they want to engage with us? How do they want to engage with us? These are the questions modern retailers must consider in order to remain culturally relevant.

In Pacsun's case, it's become increasingly clear that what our consumers want is authentic, engaging experiences. That applies whether those experiences are happening on- or offline. And we've discovered that those experiences are more meaningful to our community when they are informed by purpose.

PURPOSE INFORMS AUTHENTIC CONSUMER EXPERIENCES, ONLINE OR OFF

I truly believe that modern brands need purpose to thrive—maybe even to survive. Purpose is what transforms transactions into relationships, building brand-loyal communities that don't just buy from a brand but champion it. Without purpose, even the coolest product mix or celebrity collaboration risks becoming white noise: easy to ignore.

As Pacsun has developed its digital muscle and reframed its approach to in-person shopping, developing a truly omnichannel experience, we've learned that technology alone isn't the answer. Technology simply amplifies existing intention, and if that intention is purely transactional, not focused on relationship building, technology can't make up for that. On the other hand, when purpose leads, technology becomes a tool not only for operational efficiency but also for deeper connection. This means that purpose can't be an afterthought in the conversation; it has to lead the conversation.

CHAPTER 8

PURPOSE CAN'T BE AN AFTERTHOUGHT

PACSUN HAS PARTNERED with the Los Angeles Rams for nearly a decade. Initially, the partnership was born from the simple fact that our company and the NFL team are both headquartered in LA. However, as Pacsun developed into a more purpose-led brand, the partnership became much more meaningful. A look at how it's evolved demonstrates the power of leading with purpose.

When Pacsun first partnered with the Los Angeles Rams, we paid for a celebrity suite at the Los Angeles Memorial Coliseum, where the team played from 2016 to 2019. Pacsun would welcome influencers and celebrities to the suite, creating a bespoke, exclusive experience that they could share with their followers online. The celebrity suite experience was something covetable and exciting, and the content that was created by the influencers and celebrities who attended performed well. However, it lacked purpose. The content created buzz, but there was no "So what?" factor. What good was it doing? How were we serving the LA community? Where could we make a change? How were we inspiring our youth?

Our partnership with the Los Angeles Rams had already been ongoing for a couple of years when we started having these conversations. Ultimately, we decided that it didn't make sense to pay for the celebrity suite. Instead, we wanted to find a way to take that money and do something quietly and with intention that would build up our LA community.

We started with fun, playful things, such as having Rampage, the Los Angeles Rams mascot, deliver coolers filled with Pacsun products to people who were tailgating, parked in the stadium parking lot before games. It didn't matter whether they had tickets to the game or not. The point was to create a moment of surprise and delight: Pacsun and Rampage, showing up together for fans of the Los Angeles Rams.

Then, the Los Angeles Rams moved to SoFi Stadium in Inglewood, California. That led to a conversation with the superintendent of Inglewood schools. From him, we learned that the number one reason kids weren't making it to school was that they didn't have clean clothing. In response, Pacsun and the Los Angeles Rams have donated more than $5 million worth of apparel to over fifty thousand students throughout LA County. It felt useful and purposeful, like we were really starting to make a difference.

There was just one problem: We hadn't considered that some of the kids who were recipients of the clothes might not have access to laundry facilities. When we spoke to the superintendent of Inglewood schools months later and asked him how the partnership was going, he paused before admitting that even though the kids had new clothes, they couldn't clean them.

So, the following year, Pacsun and the Los Angeles Rams got together and thought about what we could do differently. That is when we conceptualized Loads of Love, a three-way partnership between Pacsun, the Los Angeles Rams, and Tide, that installs washers and dryers in schools. With support from the Thinkwatts Foundation, Loads of Love has provided twenty schools from the Compton Unified School District and the Los Angeles Unified School District with a washer/dryer set.[52]

The evolution of this partnership represents a fundamental shift in how Pacsun has developed its purpose. We aren't just checking a box so that we can say we did our philanthropy for the year. We are actively seeking ways to create a better future for young generations, recognizing that it starts in our own community. Sometimes, that means finding a way to support an entire school system. Other times, it's as simple as helping a single individual—such as Brendan.

Pacsun was connected with Brendan through the Make-A-Wish foundation. Brendan loves fashion, and when his wish coordinator reached out to Pacsun to see if we could grant his wish of getting a sewing machine, we wanted to do more. We gifted Brendan everything he needed to create his very own sewing space and also invited him to visit our headquarters to learn from our design team. Brendan's visit was a genuine exchange in which our designers learned from his creativity just as much as he learned from them. It was an instance of co-creation in its purest form: recognizing that inspiration and innovation can come from anywhere, including a young person who simply loves fashion.

52 "Rams & Pacsun Team Up to Combat Chronic Absenteeism in Under-Resourced Schools," TheRams.com, May 28, 2024, https://www.therams.com/news/rams-pacsun-team-up-to-combat-chronic-absenteeism-in-under-resourced-schools.

When you're creating genuine impact, everyone involved feels connected to something meaningful. For our Pacsun teams, the pride and sense of purpose such initiatives bring translates into everything we do, from how we serve customers to how we talk about our brand to how we show up in our communities. Defining Pacsun as a purpose-led brand has been the game-changer for us, with implications felt at every level.

PACSUN'S JOURNEY TO PURPOSE

Pacsun's transformation into a purpose-led brand in some ways mirrors my own career transformation. In 2019, I completed a ten-week in-person educational program at Harvard, where I was introduced to the book *True North* by Bill George and Peter Eagle Sims. The book is structured in three parts: becoming an authentic leader, discovering your authentic leadership, and empowering others. It forces you to reflect on your life story, notably the most pivotal experiences—what the authors call setbacks or crucibles—to identify what truly motivates you, which then reveals your deeper purpose, also known as your true north.

The true north is rooted in five pillars: integrity, self-awareness, courage, humility, and passion. According to George and Sims, in order to live your true north, your purpose must be intertwined with both your personal and professional lives. You can't have one purpose at home and another at work. That line of thought is what initially pointed me in the direction of purpose work.

I was then introduced to my executive coach at Case Leadership, and she introduced me to the Conscious Capitalism group. Conscious Capitalism, or Responsible Capitalism, believes that businesses fundamentally have to take a larger responsibility for creating a better world and that social responsibility is linked to corporate responsibility. The Conscious Capitalism group further confirmed that purpose-led brands deliver better business results.

This belief was further affirmed when I attended the Conscious Capitalism CEO Summit in Austin, Texas, in 2022. There, I met a couple of individuals who deepened my understanding of how purpose-driven leadership could transform not only individual companies but also entire industries. I had a particularly meaningful conversation with John Mackey, the co-founder and former CEO of Whole Foods, who helped guide the brand toward its purpose: to nourish people and the planet. I also met Doug Rauch, who spent thirty-one years at Trader Joe's and served as company president for fourteen years. Doug was instrumental in developing the Trader Joe's philosophy and creating what became known as Trader Joe's University—a leadership program focused on culture, consumer connection, and purpose-driven work.

What struck me about Doug's approach was how he had unlocked the simplicity of being guided by purpose while making that purpose crystal clear to employees. The mission of Trader Joe's is to provide customers with a unique and enjoyable grocery shopping experience, characterized by outstanding value, quality products, and friendly service. Doug shared how hiring friendly people became the crucible of creating that consistent in-store experience customers have come to love. Doug's message was simple, but it really hit home: Purpose must be alive and felt within all aspects of the organization, most importantly on the front lines with the consumer.

When I stepped into Pacsun's CEO role in 2023, I saw an opportunity to more broadly implement my vision of Pacsun as a purpose-led brand. I wasn't alone in wanting to take this path. Many people at Pacsun shared my enthusiasm for leading with purpose and were already doing great work toward that end. Still, if we wanted to pivot the company in a more concrete, far-reaching way, we had to get board buy-in. As the new CEO, it was my job to communicate to the board the new vision we'd developed for the company—and to then convince them that our belief in a purpose-led company made sense from a business standpoint as well as a cultural one.

The executive team went into that board meeting with a clear vision to present: We no longer wanted to be known for curating the best brands and products; we wanted to be known for leading with purpose and inspiring the next generation of youth. We prepared our business case, citing examples of purpose-led companies that have stood the test of time. Think of Patagonia, a company dedicated to saving our home planet, or Nike, which aims to bring inspiration and innovation to every athlete, or LEGO, which strives to inspire and develop the builders of tomorrow.

There is no shortage of data to back up the assertion that purpose-led companies perform better. Here is a small overview:

- According to researchers from Harvard Business School, firms exhibiting both high purpose and clarity achieved significantly higher future accounting and stock market performance, even after controlling for current baseline performance.[53]
- McKinsey, drawing on work by Raj Sisodia, reports that purpose-led companies significantly outperformed the S&P 500 index in the period 1996 to 2011.[54]

---

53 Claudine Gartenberg et al., "Corporate Purpose and Financial Performance," *Organization Science* 30, no. 1 (2019): 1–18, https://www.hbs.edu/faculty/Pages/item.aspx?num=54523.

54 Arne Gast et al., "Purpose: Shifting from Why to How," *McKinsey Quarterly*, April 22, 2020, https://www.mckinsey.com/capabilities/people-and-organizational-performance/our-insights/purpose-shifting-from-why-to-how.

- A Kantar Consulting survey suggests that purposeful brands grow more than twice as fast as their competition.[55]
- According to Deloitte, purpose-led companies see higher market share gains and grow three times faster on average than their competitors.[56]
- A global Zeno Group study suggests that consumers are four times more likely to purchase from a company that they see as having a strong purpose and six times more likely to protect that same company in the event of a misstep or public criticism.[57]
- According to McKinsey, 83 percent of Gen Z say they choose brands that align with their values.[58]
- A WGSN report on Gen Alpha trends reveals that 64 percent of Gen Alpha expect brands to actively take part in solving social and environmental issues.[59]
- Pacsun's 2025 Youth Report highlights just how important purpose is to younger consumers. Survey respondents were asked: "When you think about what mental health means to

---

55 Afdhel Aziz, "The Power of Purpose: Kantar Purpose 2020 Study Shows How Purposeful Brands Grow Twice as Fast as Their Competition," *Forbes*, November 11, 2019, https://www.forbes.com/sites/afdhelaziz/2019/11/11/the-power-of-purpose-kantar-purpose-2020-study-shows-how-purposeful-brands-grow-twice-as-fast-as-their-competition/.

56 Livia Zufferli, "2020 Global Marketing Trends: Bringing Authenticity to Our Digital Age," Deloitte, December 1, 2020, https://www.deloitte.com/ca/en/services/consulting/perspectives/global-marketing-trends-2020.html.

57 "Unveiling The 2020 Zeno Strength of Purpose Study," Zeno Group, June 17, 2020, https://www.zenogroup.com/insights/2020-zeno-strength-purpose.

58 "What Is Gen Z?," McKinsey & Company, last updated August 28, 2024, https://www.mckinsey.com/featured-insights/mckinsey-explainers/what-is-gen-z.

59 "Gen Alpha Trends," WGSN, https://www.wgsn.com/en/wgsn-gen-alpha-trends.

> you personally, how important are each of the following?" The response "Feeling like I have a purpose" resonated with many, with 37% of respondents deeming this "extremely important" and an additional 31% deeming it "very important." Young people are clearly seeking purpose. What if a brand can help them discover it?

Those facts and figures are undeniably impactful. However, I think what won the board over wasn't hard data but a deeper understanding of how Pacsun could inspire true brand love by leading with purpose. To make this case, we presented a series of videos that our team had created through consumer research—essentially, customer intercepts where we asked people a simple question: "What does Pacsun mean to you?" The responses were incredibly emotional and visceral. One person stated, "Pacsun has always been a safe space." Another said, "I felt the most expressed, the most happy, and the most out of my comfort zone in your guys' clothing." Others talked about how Pacsun represented freedom, creativity, and authentic self-expression.

As board meetings go, this was one where the nerves were palpable. These insights had been percolating within the company, but they hadn't been clearly articulated as a strategic direction. The consumer reactions in that video provided the clarity we needed, demonstrating the power we had as a brand to transform how people saw themselves and their place in the world. The board members agreed, confirming that our vision of a purpose-led Pacsun was worth pursuing. It was a pivotal moment that gave us the conviction to move forward 100 percent on this path.

ARTICULATING PACSUN'S PURPOSE

With a firmly aligned leadership team and board buy-in, Pacsun was firmly able to step fully into its vision of being a purpose-led company that serves its community. Pacsun's purpose pillars articulated the new direction clearly, and we still refer to these today. According to these pillars, Pacsun is:

1. **Culture-first:** We don't just follow trends. We help shape them. Pacsun is deeply rooted in youth culture, curating fashion, music, and experiences that reflect the voices of Gen Z and Gen Alpha. Our brand is a platform on which creativity, individuality, and cultural expression come to life through the lens of emerging creators, artists, and athletes. Culture is not a marketing tool for us. It's our operating system.
2. **Community-centric:** At the heart of Pacsun is a belief in co-creation. From our Youth Advisory Council to our purpose-driven partnerships, we invite our community to build with us, not just shop with us. We prioritize representation, dialogue, and connection with the people who inspire us most: our customers. We don't just speak to our audience; we build with them.
3. **Purpose-driven:** We believe brands have a responsibility to stand for something more. Pacsun invests in sustainability, mental wellness, inclusion, and social impact, not as a side campaign but as a core business priority. Our Purpose Partner Summit, brand collaborations, and nonprofit initiatives are designed to create measurable, lasting change. Purpose is not a project. It's our promise.

4. **Future-facing:** From TikTok Shop to Web3 experiments, Pacsun leads where youth and innovation converge. We're reimagining what retail means through immersive commerce, creator-led storytelling, and global expansion. The future of fashion lives at the intersection of digital, community, and culture. We move at the speed of Gen Z and sometimes faster.

With the purpose pillars as our guide, we were able to dive deeper and think about how to actually enact and live those pillars, not only for ourselves but also for our community. We began by identifying four driving forces of youth culture: fashion, music, art, and sport. Of course, there are other things you might put on that list, such as gaming. Those four things are not the *only* things driving youth culture. However, they are four things truly integral to youth culture. Just as importantly, they create beautiful synergies between them.

You can see this interconnectedness reflected in our 2025 Youth Report. Music, for instance, is the number one way young people address their mental health. When they're not feeling themselves, they'll listen to a certain song, and it can completely change their mood. Meanwhile, sports create equity and have the power to transform lives through movement and inclusion. Art serves as a pillar of self-expression, whether that's traditional fine art, tattoo art, or the countless other ways people express creativity beyond just museums. Finally, fashion becomes the canvas for all of this expression—how young people choose to present themselves to the world, influenced by the music they love, the art that inspires them, and the sports that move them. These aren't separate categories; they're interconnected elements of how people in our community live, create, and connect with each other.

Pacsun's initiatives are now designed to thoughtfully align with at least one of these four youth culture driving forces. This strategic framework has transformed how we approach everything from product design to event planning to creator collaborations. When we show up at music festivals, launch athletic wear lines, partner with artists, or collaborate with designers, it's intentional. Each effort strengthens our commitment to our purpose: Pacsun seeks to inspire the next generation of youth, building community at the intersection of fashion, music, art, and sport.

Fashion: We Innovate

Pacsun leads through creativity and pushes the frontiers of design with many of the creative partnerships I've already mentioned, from our A$AP Rocky collaboration to our work with Japanese fashion designer Yohji Yamamoto. Beyond that, we also encourage our community to get involved, nurturing the next generation of design innovators.

Pacsun's 2021 Gender-Neutral Design Competition with the Fashion Scholarship Fund and the aspiring student designers in the program, as mentioned in chapter 4, is a perfect example. This was motivated by our recognition of the increasingly fluid approach to gender taken by Generations Alpha and Z and a desire to offer them a fitting outlet for expression. The winners, Allegra Abrams and Oli Carrillo, worked with and were mentored by our design and production teams to create their very own gender-neutral collections, which launched in Pacsun stores in spring 2022.

The PS Hub has further empowered future creators, allowing our community members to exchange creative ideas—for example, by giving aspiring designers the chance to upload their concepts for community feedback and get potential partnership opportunities with Pacsun. With such initiatives, the goal is to create opportunities for the next generation of designers and give them a platform for their creative vision.

Often, that creative vision is accompanied by a purposeful vision. Take Reese Cooper's RC Outdoor Supply (RCOS) line, for example, which was made possible with Pacsun's support. Inspired by his appreciation of the beauty and inclusiveness of California's outdoor culture, the origin of the RCOS collection traces back to late 2021, when Cooper began quietly developing a line of outdoor products in addition to his runway collections. Founded on a shared enthusiasm for adventure and the outdoors, Cooper and Pacsun saw an opportunity to make Cooper's design aesthetic accessible to the Pacsun community. Proceeds from the collection go to One Tree Planted, which aims to restore natural wildlife habitats.

LESSON LEARNED: Innovating in fashion is about investing in the future. That means investing in up-and-coming talents, such as Allegra Abrams and Oli Carrillo, while also investing in the world they will inherit. By supporting causes such as One Tree Planted, we take a step in that direction. Platforms such as PS Hub have democratized this process even further, allowing anyone with a creative vision to potentially become our next collaborator. And perhaps there will be a framework that allows them to donate proceeds to a charity of their choice.

Music: We Co-Create

Pacsun's approach to music centers on partnering with artists to shape the brand together, moving beyond traditional sponsorships to genuine creative collaboration. A$AP Rocky's role as guest artistic director exemplified this, but equally important was our work with Willow Smith on our Colour Range collection debut—our first truly unisex, gender-free line. Willow's ethos aligned perfectly with where our community was heading at that time. In addition to endorsing and wearing the collection, she performed in our store, creating an intimate experience that connected music, fashion, and authentic self-expression.

Our music partnerships now extend to major festivals where we create lasting emotional connections rather than temporary brand exposure. At Outside Lands in San Francisco, for example, Pacsun brought its 2025 festival tour to Golden Gate Park, celebrating the vibrant connection between live music, self-expression, and community. From our pop-up store to a festival-exclusive capsule collection featuring limited-edition unisex pieces, we created a space for fans to explore the intersection of LA style and the eclectic energy of the festival. Each piece was a collector's item tied to a moment, a place, and a shared experience.

Our approach at Governors Ball similarly demonstrated how we integrate music experiences with our broader community strategy. We kicked things off with a "Get Ready with Pacsun" event at our SoHo flagship store, where fans lined up for festival fits, a live DJ set, tooth gems, drinks, and chances to win free Converse and Gov Ball tickets. The energy in the store was incredible—it showed how our physical retail spaces can serve as launching pads for cultural moments. At the festival itself, our Pacsun Festival Hub featured an exclusive Gov Ball × Pacsun collaborative apparel collection, key festival styles, a glam booth with Rare Beauty, limited edition totes for Apple Pay users, and interactive photo opportunities. We also hosted content creators and friends of the brand who shared their experiences throughout the festival weekend, creating authentic peer-to-peer advocacy rather than traditional brand messaging.

LESSON LEARNED: Music partnerships work best when they feel like natural extensions of our community's lifestyle rather than forced brand insertions. By focusing on memory-making rather than mass merchandising, we create lasting emotional connections that extend beyond the event. When those memories are shared with others, they become a powerful catalyst for community.

Art: We Inspire

Pacsun's efforts in the arts are all about sparking creativity. Our Pacsun Collective is a prime example, bringing together people across many fields—content creators, photographers, videographers, stylists, designers, musicians, and digital artists—to join Pacsun's creative process and help shape future campaigns and merchandise. Our Spring/Summer 2024 Campaign was co-created with the brand's in-house creative team and a curated selection of such community visionaries.

Our commitment to inspiring through art is also seen in our partnerships with names such as The Metropolitan Museum of Art. At the same time, we believe that something doesn't need to be housed in a museum to be seen as art. That's why we make a point of celebrating creativity in all its forms, from street graffiti to tattoo art.

Take our collaboration with Brendan Monroe, part of our Pac Artist Network Series. An LA-based artist known for his connection to graffiti culture, Monroe's mural work transforms surfaces with curved, biomorphic lines that resonate with human scale and nature. Drawn to the amorphous shapes of nature, he captures motion through line, dimension, and negative space. We celebrated our launch of the Brendan Monroe Collection with a live window painting activation at Pacsun's downtown LA flagship store, giving fans and the local community a firsthand look at his artistic process.

Monroe is only one of many artists we've collaborated with through the Pac Artist Network Series, which is our way of spotlighting visionary creators and giving them a platform to share their work in ways that feel both culturally relevant and deeply personal. In addition to our collaboration with Monroe, we've worked with Kelly Malka, an LA-born artist known for her vibrant and playful style that captures the essence of her hometown, and Randy Perez, founder and creative director of Uuuntld. Perez's hand-drawn designs—inspired by equestrian culture, strength, and motion—bring a fresh perspective to our community, blending fine art, fashion, and cultural symbolism.

LESSON LEARNED: Art isn't confined to galleries and museums—it's everywhere our community expresses themselves, from street murals to social media posts and the way people style our clothes. By celebrating creativity in all its forms, we position ourselves as champions of authentic self-expression rather than gatekeepers of what counts as art.

Sport: We Take Action

Our partnership with the Los Angeles Rams is just one example of how we are collaborating in the sports space. We've also partnered with Angel City FC of the National Women's Soccer League on a product collection, set for release in 2026, and a community activation to benefit the Las Fotos Project. Las Fotos was launched to elevate the voices of teenage girls and gender-expansive youth from communities of color through photography and mentoring, empowering them to channel their creativity for the benefit of themselves, their community, and their future careers.

Pacsun has also created a series of product collections with the LAFC, and together, we have supported Bresee Youth Center in its annual backpack drive. Bresee's mission is to battle poverty by empowering youth and families in LA with the skills, resources, and relationships necessary to thrive. This gives us the chance to help kids in our local community, donating backpacks and clothing for the back-to-school season.

With our sports pillar, we further want to cement the Pacsun brand in movement, inclusion, and physicality. With that in mind, we look for ways to get our community active, for example, by collaborating with Newport Run Club and inviting members to meet in our stores. It's astounding to see how many kids show up, and we've started creating custom merch for each run club with their specific group name on it. The point isn't to monetize the moment but to *create* that personalized, special moment in the first place: the kind of moment that makes people feel seen and heard, and eager to return.

LESSON LEARNED: Whatever the size of a partnership, whether it's with a nationally recognized sports team or a local charity, these collaborations allow amazing moments of advocacy to happen. When we outfit run club members in our new A.R.C. and PAC 1980 activewear lines, we're building microcommunities that become powerful advocates for our brand and, potentially, for the change they want to see in their local area.

PUTTING PURPOSE INTO ACTION

Articulating a purpose is one thing. Putting it into action is another. In this chapter, I've detailed some of the partnerships and initiatives that helped Pacsun achieve our dream of becoming a truly purposeful brand. What this chapter doesn't show is the huge amount of effort that went into realizing those endeavors. Many passionate, dedicated people helped make those things happen, from our own Pacsun employees to members of our community and brand partners.

By the time the executive team presented its vision for a purpose-led Pacsun to the board, we had already tested out various purpose-led initiatives. Once we got the buy-in from the board, we had the freedom to lean into this new vision and develop a comprehensive approach that touched every aspect of our operations, from how we hired and promoted talent to how we measured success and made strategic decisions.

We couldn't just develop a new mission statement and expect that to result in the cultural shift we were after. We had to put a framework in place to put purpose into action—because if you don't operationalize purpose, you aren't really living it, and that lack of authenticity is only going to hurt your company and your brand.

CHAPTER 9

CULTURE AS AN OPERATING SYSTEM

IF YOU WANT to see Pacsun's purpose in action, just look at our campaigns. In August 2025, Pacsun brought its new denim collection to life in Jackson Hole, Wyoming, with experiences ranging from horseback rides to line dancing alongside some of Gen Z's most influential voices. More than a campaign, this was co-creation in action: authentic, immersive, and community driven. The results spoke to the success of that approach, as the campaign reached upwards of eighty-five million people. That's the magic that can happen when you have real voices sharing real experiences in real time.

A similarly magical moment was evident in our 2023 holiday campaign—one of our first campaigns to launch following our decision to lead with purpose. The campaign was conceptualized as a celebration of the diverse stories and styles that make up our vibrant community, reflecting our ethos of inclusivity and giving back. To create the campaign, we invited store employees, customers, and online followers to submit video entries for a chance to be featured. The response was astounding. We received thousands of entries reflecting our diverse community. In the end, we selected twenty-nine of them to participate in the campaign and video, bringing each individual's story to life.

The point was to put our community in the spotlight. The result was a testament to the power that comes with co-creating, allowing our consumers to not only see themselves represented in our brand story but also actively shape that narrative through their own authentic voices and experiences. The slogan summed it up perfectly: "This is Y(our) Story." Because it wasn't just the Pacsun story. It was the story of our community too. As we've embraced co-creation, those two stories have become inextricably linked in a very powerful way—a way that inspires true brand love.

Campaigns such as these embody the transformation that Pacsun has gone through, revealing how our customer-centric, purpose-led approach has become second nature, something that is only possible when internal and external forces align. That requires a foundation of shared values as well as cohesive systems through which those values can be lived. We're no longer looking at individual change initiatives but acting out embedded cultural practices—and the resulting outputs, campaigns such as these, have received overwhelmingly positive feedback as a result.

When we invite our customers to co-create with us, we are also demonstrating a spirit of inclusivity that we've found really resonates with today's youth. We invite anyone who loves Pacsun to champion the brand, regardless of race, gender, religion, geographic origin, or anything else. All are welcome. This spirit of inclusivity has become a point of connection between Pacsun and its community—and we are seeing the excitement about that kind of inclusivity beyond Pacsun as well.

In 2025, for instance, The Gap released a campaign for its denim featuring KATSEYE, a girl group whose members represent different nationalities, ethnicities, and cultural backgrounds from around the world, from the Philippines to South Korea, Switzerland, and the US. The ad was celebrated for its diversity. As one media outlet put it: "The diversity, dancing and fashion has helped the ad go viral at a time when there's been debate about how companies are relating to their customer base."[60]

The KATSEYE campaign demonstrates a broader industry shift: Brands are recognizing that today's consumers expect to see themselves reflected authentically in brand narratives. This isn't about representation for representation's sake but about understanding that modern youth culture is inherently diverse. By listening to our consumers and including them in our creative process—as with the "This is Y(our) Story" holiday campaign—Pacsun aims to remain a brand that reflects the actual diversity of our community rather than an idealized or narrow version of it.

This commitment to authentic dialogue is exactly why we built the Pacsun Collective, inviting members of our community, from content creators to digital artists, photographers, and more, to join us in co-creating our brand. The Collective was created with the belief that inspiring the next generation and building the future of the Pacsun brand go hand in hand.

Our proprietary community hub, PS Hub, takes this to the next level. This interactive platform allows our community to exchange

60 Lisa Respers France, "In America's Denim Divide, Katseye Delivered a Moment That's as Comfy as an Old Pair of Jeans," *CNN Entertainment*, August 26, 2025, https://edition.cnn.com/2025/08/25/entertainment/katseye-gap-ad.

creative ideas and opinions. For example, aspiring designers can upload their ideas for community feedback and get potential partnership opportunities with Pacsun. It's a space where our community can go beyond passive consumption and actively contribute, collaborate, and help shape what Pacsun will become.

By staying attentive to our consumer base and engaging with them in real, meaningful dialogue on the topics that matter to them, we can continue to promote a spirit of authentic co-creation and inclusivity. That kind of shift is only possible when it's supported by equally intentional transformation on the inside.

OPERATIONALIZING PURPOSE: A SHIFT IN COMPANY CULTURE

Moments such as that 2023 holiday campaign are not made possible by a single person. They require a collective effort, backed by an aligned purpose. When we made the decision to take Pacsun in a purpose-driven direction, we knew we had to bring that sense of purpose to life throughout the entire organization. The question we faced was this: How do you get everyone on board with what our purpose means and how we operate and then scale and amplify that understanding throughout the entire organization? It required a fundamental shift in our organizational culture.

Today, we view culture as an operating system. While our pillars of fashion, music, art, and sport serve as organizing principles across functions, we further operationalize our five values (people, integrity, passion, innovation, teamwork) through our internal processes and frameworks.

People: Empowering Employees

When we introduced Pacsun's purpose, we already had so many people at Pacsun who were genuinely excited about the brand and their place in its ecosystem. How could we invite them to truly co-create the brand's future with us in a meaningful way? The answer lay in creating pathways for authentic career growth that prioritized purpose alignment over traditional credentials.

We have built an incredible pipeline for bringing store employees—our field team and best brand ambassadors—into our headquarters and developing them throughout the organization. For example, our head of stores started in a Cincinnati location; fifteen years later, he's now the VP overseeing all field operations. Our head of women's divisional merchandising started as an intern who had worked in stores. These aren't isolated examples. There are many more, and cumulatively, they represent a deliberate strategy.

Pacsun has become known for promoting from within. We believe in people who believe in our mission, who care deeply about our customers, and who want to be part of our community. We can provide the leadership training a person needs to advance, but we can't provide them with a sense of purpose if it isn't there in the first place. Do they care deeply about the Pacsun community? That is what matters to us.

Since 2023, Pacsun has ramped up its investment in employee training and development. We started with twelve senior leaders, then expanded to seventy-five key leaders in the organization. At a 2024 leadership retreat, we began by aligning on collective intentions and then developing a road map for how to get there. We discussed everything from taking pauses for affirmation and appreciation to identifying strengths and weaknesses and figuring out how to have tough conversations. Each leader built their own development jumpstart, a custom development plan with specific action steps. We're now scaling this work to our field teams so that everyone is speaking the same language and our culture grows cohesively.

One of the most powerful tools we've implemented is called the Merlin exercise—a vision exercise in which leaders write down their thoughts before bed in response to questions like: "You wake up in 2030 or 2035—what does Pacsun look like? What are you proud of? What's your vision for the company?" We brought in a leadership coach to work alongside me to push people to think differently and bigger about what our vision could mean, not just culturally but from a revenue standpoint as well. The investment has paid off. When leaders at every level understand and embody our purpose, they become empowered to make decisions that align with our mission, creating a multiplier effect throughout the organization.

LESSON LEARNED: Hiring for purpose alignment creates a stronger foundation than hiring for credentials alone. Skills can be taught, but genuine care for your community cannot. When you prioritize internal promotion and create clear pathways for growth, you're building a team of empowered people who understand your brand from the ground up.

Integrity: Delivering Good, Driven by Purpose

Whether it's encouraging our corporate teams to develop new partnership ideas or inspiring our store employees to get involved in local charities, we try to equip them with the means they need to succeed. That means leading with integrity and encouraging them to do the same.

Our work with national nonprofit Delivering Good is a great example of this. Since 1985, Delivering Good has been connecting individuals and families who face poverty, homelessness, and disasters with new products that open doors to hope, dignity, and opportunity. By connecting with manufacturers, community partners, and retailers (such as Pacsun), Delivering Good ensures that donated products have a meaningful impact on the lives they reach.

For example, at the end of each season, a Pacsun store manager can look at their local community's needs and decide where they want their clothing donations to go. They might choose a women's shelter, a homeless shelter, or a mental health organization. They package up the goods themselves, write handwritten notes, and personally deliver the items to the charity of their choice.

Initiatives such as this give our teams personal agency over the purpose they are working toward. It's so much more meaningful than if Pacsun's corporate headquarters were to write a blank check to a charity. This isn't to say that type of charitable giving is bad. It's just not as likely to unify Pacsun employees at large with that sense of satisfaction that comes with doing good and leading with integrity.

LESSON LEARNED: By giving store associates the agency to decide which local charities receive donations, we're allowing them to create meaningful connections with their respective communities. When you encourage employees to lead with integrity in this way, it creates a sense of pride and ownership that translates into stronger employee retention and authentic brand advocacy.

Passion: Speaking Up and Encouraging Others to Do the Same

A sense of shared purpose is incredibly powerful. Both motivating and inspiring, it can spark real passion. We've seen it ourselves in how our community, both internally and externally, responds to our purpose-driven initiatives. When proceeds for a product go to a good cause, our customers rally behind it. When we highlight a charitable initiative, our community gets curious about it. And when we use our platform to articulate not only our purpose but also the values that underpin it, our Pacsun people are chiming in, adding their voices to the conversation.

Consider, for example, the June 2025 protests in LA. The protests began after Immigration and Customs Enforcement agents raided several city locations to arrest individuals allegedly involved in illegal immigration to the US. In the face of these protests, there was a move to federalize the California National Guard, and some two thousand guard members were deployed to the city.

On June 10, 2025, Pacsun posted an image with the following text on Instagram: "At Pacsun, we believe the heart of our community lies in the people and cultures that shape this vibrant, diverse city. Right now, so many are feeling unsure or afraid, but we want you to know: We are with you, Los Angeles."[61] Here is a small sampling of the responses in the comment section: "i love u pacsun," "WOWOWOWOWOW PACSUN JUST GOT MY MONEY," "Yeahhh I'll be shopping at pacsun moving forward >>>>>," "Ladies, looks like we'll be shopping at PACSUN from now on." And finally: "I love working for this company."

Pacsun is passionate about leading with purpose, and we want our employees to share in that passion. Having someone post publicly that they *love* working for the company because we were vocal in speaking out against actions that go against our values? That's a true testament to the passion of our employees. And it all comes back to our purpose.

---

61 Pacsun (@pacsun), "we are with you, Los Angeles," Instagram post, June 10, 2025, https://www.instagram.com/pacsun/p/DKusmKmxnnK/.

LESSON LEARNED: When your brand takes authentic stands on issues that matter to your community, your employees become proud advocates rather than just workers. The response to those moments when Pacsun shows community support creates emotional investment at every level of the organization. Passion can't be manufactured through corporate messaging. It requires people feeling that their workplace reflects their values.

Innovation: Embracing Outside-the-Box Thinking

Much of Pacsun's success in its journey to reclaim cultural relevance has come from its unconventional approaches. We got on TikTok when it was still only known as a dance app, for example, and invited creators to tell our story while other brands maintained a strong hold on their narratives. It should thus come as no surprise that we encourage our employees to think outside the box themselves.

One example of this innovative spirit is how Pacsun has been popping up in places outside of traditional retail without the help of external agencies. We're trackside at Formula 1 races, ringside at Ultimate Fighting Championship events, and in the crowd at Outside Lands and Gov Ball, and we do it all with our own internal teams. This really comes down to passion, people, and teamwork because it's not easy to plan and execute these kinds of fleeting event experiences. But our local store employees, alongside our brand marketing teams, show up and pull it together, setting up temporary storefronts, lugging products on-site, and more.

This is what it looks like when culture truly becomes your operating system and everyone is putting the customer first. Instead of saying, "Oh, there's this really cool opportunity, but it's also a ton of work, so let's hire an outside team to handle it," we empower our people to bring these experiences to life together, leaning into the cultural moment we are building alongside our community. Our teams are enthusiastic about what they're doing because they helped to create the experiences, and that enthusiasm helps team retention. It also translates to the customer.

LESSON LEARNED: When employees are empowered to think beyond their job descriptions and contribute to ambitious projects, they develop ownership and enthusiasm that translates directly to customer experiences. This approach is more cost-effective than hiring agencies, but more importantly, it builds internal capabilities and cultural confidence that compound over time.

Teamwork: Recognizing the Collective Effort

I've already written about our internal evolution from a competitive, individualistic culture to a more collaborative one, as evidenced in things such as our brand promise, which includes the statement "We win as a team."[62] With that said, words alone are not enough to change how people relate to a company or to one another within it. We also made adjustments to tangibles such as bonus structures, shifting from a discretionary individual bonus model to team-based bonuses that any employee (not just management) is eligible for.

The customer may be at the center of all Pacsun does, but it's our teams that shine the spotlight on them—and we don't take that for granted. When we hosted our Pacsun Purpose Summit in September 2025, for example, we didn't just invite customers, brands, and celebrity partners. We also invited Pacsun employees from our headquarters, as well as our top seventy-five store managers and our field leadership

62 Pacsun, "Who We Are."

team, flying everyone in from across the country. The Summit was a testament to their success, and we wanted them to feel that.

LESSON LEARNED: Real teamwork requires consistent reinforcement through actions, not just policies. Our field teams are on the front lines with our customers and in our community every day, so when they attend major events such as our Purpose Summit, we're showing them that their contributions are essential to our success story. True teamwork emerges when everyone understands how their role connects to the larger mission.

FROM CONTROL TO CO-CREATION: THE NEW OPERATING SYSTEM

Pacsun is a case study in how co-creation can revitalize a brand. To be clear, co-creation isn't just a buzzword or a campaign slogan. It's an operating system for relevance, and that operating system needs to be adopted internally if it's going to work externally.

Think of it like upgrading from a closed, proprietary operating system to an open-source platform. The old model was like running everything through a central processor. Every decision, every creative choice, every brand message had to be approved and controlled by headquarters. But that system can't handle the speed and complexity of modern culture. The co-creation operating system works more like a distributed network. Instead of all processing happening in one place, you have multiple nodes (customers, creators, employees, community members) contributing computing power to make the whole system stronger. The collective output is far more powerful than that of a single processor.

This co-creation model is one that any company can emulate if it's willing to let go of total control of its brand narrative. That seems to be the sticking point for many companies today: Even as consumers become more empowered through tools such as social media, many companies continue to cling to control, hoping to force a brand narrative from the top down instead of building it collectively from the ground up.

For those brands that *are* willing to invite their consumers to co-create, opportunities abound. The tech tools and platforms that are democratizing the media space are making it easier than ever for brands to connect with their audiences. Throughout this book, I've broken down our road map to show how we made it work for us. To summarize, here's a brief breakdown:

1. **Listen at scale:** From social listening to style leader feedback, Pacsun started seeing success when it started listening to its consumers.
2. **Establish authentic partnerships:** By embracing collaborations with individuals, brands, and community members who have a real love for Pacsun, we were able to generate true excitement about the brand.
3. **Meet your audience where they're at:** Pacsun got on TikTok before many other brands because that's where our audience was connecting, and we wanted to connect with them. Similarly, as younger generations return to malls, we've followed suit.
4. **Lead with purpose:** Articulate a purpose and then stand by it, loud and proud. Pacsun's purpose guides everything we do, from who we partner with to what kinds of charities we support and what we post on social media.

5. **Operationalize culture:** Make co-creation part of your brand DNA, inside and out. It's not a one-off tactic.

We have seen this model work for us—and we intend to continue on this path. We can't foresee all the technological changes and market developments that will come our way in the future. However, if we stick to this blueprint, I am confident that Pacsun will continue to see success.

If you're considering a brand transformation of your own, I encourage you to take a step back and honestly assess where you are versus where you want to be. Don't let the fear of change keep you stuck in patterns that no longer serve you or your audience. The first step is acknowledging that transformation is possible. Pacsun was a legacy brand with years of baggage, some good and some bad, yet we managed to reclaim our identity and what we stood for. In short: If we can do it, so can you. Here are a few questions to get you started:

- What part of your brand's identity no longer serves your future?
- Where are you over-relying on legacy?
- What does your company know about the next generation—and how are you sharing it?
- Are your internal systems built for relevance, or just control?
- What voices are you missing in your products, storytelling, or leadership?

This last point highlights the most important thing of all: listening to your consumers. Not just listening to them but engaging with them in active, honest dialogue. That is essential for genuine co-creation to happen. It requires letting go of some control, which can mean going beyond your comfort zone. However, in my experience, what you give up in control will come back to you tenfold in terms of engagement, enthusiasm, and affinity for your brand.

If your brand is dedicated to youth culture, you can start listening with one simple step: reading the Youth Report we released at Pacsun's 2025 Purpose Summit. The QR code below will take you to it. We plan to continue releasing this report about the state of the youth annually. The results are incredibly interesting. From the 2025 survey alone, we learned about everything from Gen Z's and Gen Alpha's primary influences (they're reluctant to be molded by external factors) to their use of AI tools (males are more likely to use ChatGPT regularly) and their views on relationships (healthy relationships are considered very important for mental health).

Our goal for the Youth Report is to develop a broader understanding of younger generations, which is why we've made it openly accessible to anyone who wants it. Our plan is for this to become a free annual resource for the entire industry, serving as a tool for brands, media, and industry executives to better connect with younger generations. The report cements Pacsun's role as a thought leader in youth culture, providing insight into the values, behaviors, and cultural forces shaping the lives of Gen Z and Gen Alpha. This all dovetails back to our aim to help give youth culture a platform, a way of being seen, heard, and understood.

Of course, the Youth Report will also serve as a guiding light for us at Pacsun. However, because our teams are already so effective at listening to our consumers, we found that the first iteration of the report didn't present many surprises. It mostly validated things we already knew. It was the people outside of Pacsun who had more of an aha moment when the report was published.

That aha moment confirmed to us that there is still a lot of work that needs to be done in bridging the gap between younger generations and the industries that seek to serve them. This gap represents both a challenge and an opportunity for forward-thinking brands. The companies that will thrive in the coming years are those that realize that cracking the code on youth culture means engaging directly, authentically, and consistently. And the cool thing is that once you put in the work and build trust with that generation of passionate and involved young people, they will show up for you—and they will show you real love.

BUILDING A BRAND PEOPLE LOVE

Throughout this book, I've shared Pacsun's transformation story, as I lived it. Nothing is more convincing than lived experience, and I firmly believe that Pacsun's co-creation model was the ultimate game-changer for the brand. By inviting our community to create with us, we've delivered on what they really want and need. By listening intently to them and acting on that feedback, we've established trust. By engaging with them in real, exciting ways, we've sparked their enthusiasm. And by leading with purpose, speaking and acting on our shared values, we've shown them that we *mean* it when we say we want to shape a better future for today's youth.

This has been a years-long process. In a way, it had to be: You can't earn trust overnight, and you can't achieve cultural credibility with just one or two cool events or celebrity partnerships. It takes sustained action over time, showing up again and again to meet your customers where they're at. That's how you build lasting brand love.

Now that we've built that authentic brand love, we are seeing it everywhere. We see it in the enthusiasm for our activations, in the ways our limited-edition drops sell out, and in our social media comments. Sometimes, unexpectedly, we see it on the red carpet—which is what happened when I met Kai Cenat, a well-known streamer and YouTuber, at the 2025 Grammy Awards. At the time of this writing, Kai is the third most-followed Twitch streamer, with 20 million followers. When we were introduced, his reaction was huge: "You're the CEO of Pacsun?! Let me get some free clothes! … That's my drip! I love Pacsun!"[63] He was truly authentic and exuberant in his enthusiasm. Someone captured the moment on video and posted it on socials, and it turned into this amazing moment of unexpected real love for Pacsun. At the time of this writing, the clip has garnered fifty million views.

That is what we want to see, on or off the red carpet. It doesn't matter if it's a Twitch streamer with millions of followers or a smaller creator such as Lyla Biggs filming content at home, as so many teens do. It's all real brand love to us: organic, authentic, and impossible to fake. More than anything else, that is Pacsun's greatest success story—a story that was co-written by the people we treat not as customers but as a community. We look forward to continuing to co-create the future with them.

63 liljupiterr (@liljupiterr), "kai cenat met the ceo of pacsun and asked her for free clothes," Instagram reel, February 6, 2025, https://www.instagram.com/reel/DFt0sY9N6fK/.

CONCLUSION

REFLECTIONS ON THE FUTURE OF RETAIL

THERE HAS BEEN a lot of speculation about the future of retail, with all kinds of prognostications, from the death of the shopping mall (something we've already seen to be false) to the end of traditional e-commerce (which some suggest will be replaced almost entirely by social selling). As a legacy brand that has stood the test of time, Pacsun is a testament to the fact that longevity in retail is possible, whatever the circumstances—provided you are prepared to evolve with your customer.

The company was established before the internet was mainstream and online shopping was even a thing. Initially, Pacsun existed exclusively in the form of brick-and-mortar stores, catering strongly to a limited vision of surf-and-skate culture. With time, the brand had to adapt to meet its consumers where they were. That meant expanding beyond surf and skate, stepping confidently into the digital age—first e-commerce and later social selling—and thinking strategically about what our consumers wanted and how we could best serve them.

In collaboration with our community, we came to articulate Pacsun as a purpose-led brand, created by and for youth. A lot of brilliant and passionate people rallied together to turn Pacsun into the company that it is today: co-created, culturally relevant, and competitive. The question then becomes: What next?

Ultimately, Pacsun aims to become more than a retailer. Our end goal is to become an operating system for youth culture: a platform that blends fashion, tech, and community in ways that make Pacsun impossible to copy.

The "What next?" question applies not only to Pacsun but also to retail in general. As new technologies continue to emerge and disrupt the retail space, there is no denying that the industry will fundamentally change. Some in the business see this as cause for concern. I suggest reframing it as cause for excitement. Just like Pacsun's young consumers, we believe in building a better future, and the first step of building that future is imagining it.

So, what might the future of retail look like? At Pacsun, we're already sketching out our five- and ten-year plans. While I can't share our whole playbook here, I do want to highlight some of the concepts we're contemplating:

- **Cultural network operations:** Imagine a retail brand functioning as a youth culture studio, producing content at broader scale, including for movies and television. A brand could become both a tastemaker and a platform for emerging talent.
- **AI-powered customization:** Imagine design tools that allow customers to co-create drops in minutes, with same-week

fulfillment and hyper-personalization options. Removing barriers to creative access allows for radical self-expression.

- **Retail as social utility:** Imagine stores that double as community service hubs, co-working spaces for young creatives, or mental health pop-ups. As retail goes beyond the transactional, these spaces can be used in new and exciting ways.
- **Loyalty programs reimagined:** Today, loyalty programs are still largely about perks, exclusive access, and discounts. Imagine a loyalty program reconfigured to be about community belonging. What might that look like?
- **Decentralized youth brand collective:** Imagine a network of youth-led micro brands sharing resources but operating independently, powered by blockchain creator revenue models. How do you create the LVMH of Gen Z and Gen Alpha but make it grassroots and participatory?
- **Youth accelerator programs:** Imagine a program that can discover and support emerging designers, musicians, and entrepreneurs, not only in the US but globally. Alumni from such an accelerator program can then be embedded into the cultural ecosystem.

Maybe those ideas spark some of your own. At the least, I hope they convince you that it's an incredibly exciting time to be in retail. This industry used to be about simple transactions: Give me your money, and I'll give you a product. Today, we are seeing it evolve into something much more intentional and interactional. Retail can become a space for radical personalization and authentic engagement, especially as the digital and physical retail worlds continue to blend and overlap.

We're witnessing massive shifts across every dimension: from mass to micro, from product-led to culture-led, from static operations to agile responsiveness. We are building toward a future model of retail in which authentic engagement drives everything, communities co-create rather than just consume, and brands serve as facilitators of culture rather than dictators of trends. For companies willing to embrace this evolution, the opportunities are infinite. Those who push back, on the other hand, risk becoming obsolete. Retail isn't disappearing, but brands clinging to old playbooks will.

If you're as excited about the future of retail as I am, I invite you to join the conversation on my website and our Co-Created podcast series. If my time at Pacsun has taught me anything, it's that the best ideas come from collaboration and conversation. Let's co-create the future of Pacsun—and retail at large—together.

AFTERWORD

CO-CREATED, CULTURALLY RELEVANT, AND COMPETITIVE

PEOPLE OFTEN WONDER how Pacsun managed to bounce back from bankruptcy and come back stronger than ever. This book has laid out the blueprint for how we did it—a blueprint that is adaptable and repeatable. But though the blueprint may be replicable, Pacsun offers something distinctly unique.

By reimagining Pacsun through the eyes of customers and leaning into co-creation as a competitive strategy, we have developed a brand that authentically resonates with young people in a way few others of our size do. That is seen in our purpose pillars (culture-first, community-centric, purpose-driven, and future-facing) as well as in our broader mission: to inspire the next generation of youth, building community at the intersection of fashion, music, art, and sport.

Much of this book has looked at the past—the "How we got here" story. But who are we today? What is Pacsun, now? Five key elements of our identity define us today and will guide our path to tomorrow. They are why our consumers trust us, why we continue to resonate with young people, and why we continue to grow. They are:

1. WE KNOW THE NEXT GENERATION

Whether Gen Z, Gen Alpha, or beyond, Pacsun's core audience is the most coveted consumer cohort for long-term growth. We are a rare US retailer that is native to youth culture, not chasing it. We are trusted as an authority in culture and style, which translates to impressive brand awareness—more than 70 percent in some markets.

We know the next generations because we've taken the time to get to know them. Consider some of our initiatives toward this end:

- **The Pacsun Youth Report:** As younger generations forge their way forward, Pacsun wants to be in lockstep with them—listening to their concerns, amplifying their voices, and creating platforms where they can drive meaningful change rather than simply informing our product decisions. Toward that end, we launched the Youth Report, which allows us to figure out what matters to the young people who form the basis of our community.
- **The Pacsun Youth Advisory Council:** The Youth Advisory Council aims to empower Gen Z's and Gen Alpha's authentic voices inside Pacsun. It features fifteen members aged sixteen to twenty-two from Gen Z, plus two dedicated seats for twelve- to fifteen-year-olds representing Gen Alpha voices. Council members serve one-year terms with opportunities for

renewal and internship pathways, providing advisory input across five key tracks that align with our brand pillars.

- **The Pacsun Purpose Partner Summit:** Pacsun's first Purpose Partner Summit was held in the fall of 2025, with the aim of creating a physical space where digital conversations could translate into real-world collaboration and action. The event brought together our creator community with a selection of our purpose-driven partners. Heidi Zuckerman, CEO of the Orange County Museum of Art and author of *Why Art Matters: The Bearable Lightness of Being*, spoke on why art matters to young people, for example. The event also featured a special fireside chat about music—one of the biggest drivers of youth culture—featuring participants such as Adam Roth, EVP of global partnerships and business development at The Recording Academy, and Phylicia Fant, global head of music industry and culture collaborations at Amazon Music. The feedback was so overwhelmingly positive, we plan to make it an annual event.

2. WE ARE CULTURE-LED, NOT COMMERCE-LED

Pacsun is a first mover in co-creation, partnering with creators, artists, athletes, and communities to shape our products and brand storytelling. We have deeply integrated into music, gaming, sports, and fashion ecosystems—the channels where young consumers live. Our ownable intellectual property speaks to where youth culture meets, from Roblox World Festival activations to limited-edition drops that sell out fast.

We are recognized as shaping the cultural conversation, not following it. Consider some of the organizations and individuals that Pacsun has worked with to create authentic experiences that excite and engage our community:

- **A$AP Rocky:** A$AP Rocky collaborated with Pacsun as our guest artistic director for two years, starting in 2021. He could remember shopping at Pacsun when he was younger, and he articulated a desire to bring the brand to the next generation of youth, including his own children. This wasn't just a brand collaboration for him. It meant something. In August 2021, Pacsun hosted a VIP launch party at its SoHo flagship store in New York City to celebrate the newest drop of A$AP Worldwide's collaborations with Russell Athletic and Vans. Rocky performed live. The space was packed, with crowds lining up outside to get in.
- **Governors Ball:** Our approach at Governors Ball similarly demonstrated how we integrate music experiences with our broader community strategy. We kicked things off with a "Get Ready with Pacsun" event at our SoHo flagship store, where fans lined up for festival fits, a live DJ set, tooth gems, drinks, and chances to win free Converse and Gov Ball tickets. The energy in the store was incredible; it showed how our physical retail spaces can serve as launching pads for cultural moments. At the festival itself, our Pacsun Festival Hub featured an exclusive Gov Ball × Pacsun collaborative apparel collection.
- **The Super Bowl:** In 2022, Anna Sitar and Pacsun partnered for the TikTok creator's live stream of the Super Bowl. While Sitar never explicitly mentioned the brand, she did wear a Pacsun sweatshirt. The subtle nature of the collaboration

earned accolades from advertising industry trade magazine *AdAge*. The following year, we invited Sitar to take over Pacsun's TikTok directly and host a live-stream shopping experience for our newly launched brand shop.

3. WE SEE A HUGE FINANCIAL UPSIDE, WITH ROOM TO SCALE

Pacsun has grown its digital commerce while also seeing a resurgence in brick-and-mortar traffic, with double-digit growth across all locations. We have lean, agile operations that allow us to pivot quickly to meet consumers where they are. We further have a clear white space in international markets. Our vision of the future isn't just hopeful—it's rooted in data-driven success stories. Because we know what's already working, we can move forward with confidence.

A look at more recent success stories hints at how we can expand in the future. Some highlights are:

- **TikTok Shop success:** Pacsun took an early bet on TikTok, engaging with users of the platform when it was largely considered just a dance app. That bet has paid off. At the time of this writing, in the last rolling twelve months, we've generated over $40 million in sales and sold one million pairs of jeans on TikTok Shop alone. While that's still less than 10 percent of our overall digital business, it's a significant starting point for expanding our presence. And what's most exciting is the customer data, which indicates that 95 percent of consumers we've attracted on TikTok over the past year are net new customers.

- **Super Brand Days:** Super Brand Days are promotional events on TikTok Shop where a featured brand takes center stage, offering exclusive deals, interactive content, and live shopping experiences to drive sales and brand awareness. When Pacsun participated in Super Brand Day in 2024, we became the number one seller on the platform during the four-day event, demonstrating how authentic creator relationships and strategic social commerce can drive significant business impact.
- **A rise in shopping mall foot traffic:** Shopping mall foot traffic is on the rise in general, a trend that aligns with what we're seeing at Pacsun, where we've measured a 17 percent increase in foot traffic in the past year (significantly more than the average 3 to 5 percent increase others are seeing). In Pacsun's case, that increase in foot traffic is mirrored by a boost in conversions, an indicator that our young consumers aren't just setting foot in stores but spending money while they're there.

4. WE ARE BUILT FOR THE FUTURE

Pacsun's stores are experiential hubs, not just inventory storage. E-commerce, TikTok Shop, and social commerce are deeply integrated into the way we operate. We aren't just on these platforms; they're part of our operating system. With our data-driven merchandising and trend forecasting systems, we reduce markdowns and overstock risk.

Building for the future requires building an infrastructure that is agile and data driven. Modern technology is allowing us to do just that, capitalizing on tools and tech-driven moments such as:

- **AI-powered data:** In 2025, Pacsun launched its smart platforms—MondaySmart, PlanSmart, and InventorySmart—AI-powered tools for forecasting, allocation, and buying. These systems create a dynamic way to understand what's happening in our business at any given time. We can make smarter inventory decisions, optimize allocation to specific stores, and access real-time results that previously would have taken weeks to compile.
- **Our proprietary community hub:** In fall 2025, we launched PS Hub, our own community hub. It allows us to connect with our community on our own terms, no third-party platforms needed. The platform integrates shoppable features and live social commerce capabilities.
- **The halo effect:** On Black Friday weekend 2023, Pacsun's Casey jean had a viral moment on TikTok. The cross-channel impact exceeded our projections. Beyond TikTok sales, we observed increased foot traffic in physical stores, with customers specifically requesting "the TikTok Jean," a testament to the omnichannel impact that social e-commerce can have.

5. WE STAND AT THE SWEET SPOT OF DISRUPTION

Retail isn't dead; it's transforming. Pacsun is already living that transformation. We bring together speed, agility, fashion, and brand awareness, which is why we can collaborate with institutions such as The Metropolitan Museum of Art or creators such as renowned fashion designer Yohji Yamamoto while also selling adidas, Vans, and edikted. We have a unique lane, with very little direct competition at our scale, and we have cultural credibility that can't be built overnight because it's been twenty years in the making.

Consider some of the ways we are disrupting what a traditional retailer stands for:

- **Unexpected collaborations, from McDonald's to The Met:** Pacsun's collaborations span the full spectrum of culture in a disruptive way that's rarely seen elsewhere. In fall 2023, Pacsun released its fourth collection with The Met, garnering media attention from *The New York Times*, among others. In summer 2025, Pacsun dropped its Pacsun × McDonaldland merch collection, and several pieces sold out within the first hours.
- **Local-run clubs:** Recognizing younger generations' vision of malls as shared spaces to connect, Pacsun has partnered with Newport Run Club, inviting participants to meet directly in our stores. It's astounding to see how many kids show up, and we've started creating custom merch for each run club with their own group name on it. The point isn't to monetize the moment but to make people feel seen and heard.
- **Community-based creator marketplaces:** Pacsun stores have hosted creator marketplaces, inviting local artists and small brands to do pop-ups in our stores or parking lots, with 100 percent of proceeds going back to them and a charity of their choice. These initiatives allow for the kind of community connection that sets Pacsun apart from its competitors and keeps people coming back.

If you want the kind of brand love that inspires loyalty that lasts, you need to look beyond product and consider the consumer's lifestyle as a whole. That attitude is what drives us at Pacsun.

Looking ahead, we don't just want to sell clothes—we want to become the operating system of the next generation. We invite you to join us on the journey.

ACKNOWLEDGMENTS

LIKE PACSUN ITSELF, this book is an act of co-creation, made possible thanks to the Pacsun team, our community and brand partners, and our consumers. Pacsun would not be what it is without all of you. This book is y(our) story.

More broadly, I would like to thank my Harvard Professor Rohit Deshpande for encouraging me to lead with purpose and the Conscious Capitalism group, led by John Mackey, co-founder of Whole Foods, for inspiring me to create a business for good.

ABOUT THE AUTHOR

BRIEANE OLSON is the Chief Executive Officer of Pacsun, a leading youth lifestyle retailer known for its innovative, purpose-driven brand strategy. With nearly two decades at the company, Olson has led transformational growth through bold merchandising, strategic partnerships, and a deep focus on Gen Z consumers. Her leadership reflects a modern retail mindset that blends creativity, data, and social consciousness to build relevance in an ever-evolving marketplace.

Before becoming CEO in April 2023, Olson served as President of Pacsun, where she helped redefine the brand's identity through digital-first campaigns and groundbreaking collaborations. Under her direction, Pacsun launched high-impact initiatives with cultural icons, including A$AP Rocky, Kendall and Kylie Jenner, and Jerry Lorenzo. She also oversaw the brand's international expansion into Selfridges London and the Middle East, establishing Pacsun as a global style influencer.

Olson's approach to business centers on aligning brand values with community needs. She led Pacsun's $5 million investment in inner-city Inglewood schools and developed localized outreach through the Delivering Good program, empowering store teams to make tangible, community-level change. Her ability to pair business growth with social good underscores her belief that companies thrive when they reflect and uplift the communities they serve.

With a bachelor's degree in mass communications and business from the University of California, Berkeley, and as a graduate of Harvard Business School's Advanced Management Program—where she now serves as an ambassador—Olson has built a career at the intersection of strategy, creativity, and leadership development. She has also worked with luxury fashion houses in Italy, further shaping her understanding of global brand positioning and design thinking.

Olson currently serves on the boards of Women in Retail Leadership, National Retail Federation, and Conscious Capitalism. She is a frequent speaker on purpose-driven leadership, retail innovation, and the future of consumer engagement. She lives in Southern California with her two children, Rousseau and Colette.